GET LOST!

Off-road adventures with a bicycle within easy reach of London

Patrick Field

TWO WHEELS

The author riding to third place in the Sandwich Classic at the 1994 Cycle Messenger World Championships. Photo John Williams.

Patrick Field has ridden over snow clad mountains, across hot sand deserts and - memorably - through the West Bank into Jerusalem on Palm Sunday. Despite these thrills he takes greatest pleasure in purposeless rides through the country a couple of brisk hours from his front gate.

He contributes a monthly column to *Cycling Today* and compiled and edited *Breathing Spaces - 24 bike rides within easy reach of London,* published in 1993. He runs the educational consultancy the London School of Cycling and promotes events including the legendary Dunwich Dynamo all-night ride. A founder member of the London Cycling Campaign, his political work also focuses on CHARM (Cyclists have a right to move) and the NO M11 Link Road Campaign.

He has lived in London since 1974 and divides his time between a little palace in Hackney and a time-share, tree-house in Claremont Road, Leyton.

Viva   Claremonte   Viva

First published in 1994 by

Two Wheels - an imprint of
Two Heads Publishing
12A Franklyn Suite
The Priory
Haywards Heath
West Sussex
RH16 3LB

A catalogue record for this book is available from the
British Library.

Every effort has been made to ensure the accuracy of
information in this book. Details such as Rights of Way,
tracks, roads, places to see and refreshment stops may
be subject to change and the authors and publishers
cannot accept liability for any errors or omissions.

ISBN   1-898933-15-4

Cover Design by David Spencer.
Printed & bound by Caldra House Ltd., Hove, Sussex.

CONTENTS

Page

INTRODUCTION   7

ADVENTURES REFERENCE TABLE   16

ADVENTURES LOCATION MAP
   SOUTH OF LONDON   18

ADVENTURES LOCATION MAP
   NORTH OF LONDON   19

THE ADVENTURES   21

INTRODUCTION

The Menu

These rides were chosen for a variety of reasons; splendid scenery, interesting stops and destinations, extended travel away from motor-traffic. The waterway rides are all fairly gentle, suitable for families and debutante cycle-tourists - others are more testing. The Peddars Way is included as a sample weekend expedition.

They all pass through landscapes shaped partly by nature so their character changes dramatically with the seasons. The influence of the weather on riding/grovelling conditions is - sometimes literally - staggering.

On routes that mix green roads with grey, the relative efforts involved mean that even when most of the distance is covered on smooth tarmac it is the squashy sections that give the ride its character.

Travel or Travail?

If all the tools devised by the restless invention of our species were ranked by benefit minus disadvantage, the pedal-cycle would be up there with the sewing-machine, the fiddle and the printing press. Bicycle travel is a high point of human culture, a pinnacle of our evolution.

If human organisation persists for another two hundred years the 20th Century will be regarded as a cul-de-sac where the chimeral promise of unlimited mobility offered by more complex machines briefly out-shone the bicycle's potential to increase the absolute total of human happiness. We are a long way from exhausting the diversity of this potential. We have only scratched its surface. Travel as necessity, penance or duty has a long history; recreational travel has less.

Between Earth and Air

A traveller with a bicycle engages with the shape of the land in a way that cannot be achieved by any other means. The cyclist's ability to revert to walking ('the two foot gear') gives access to all kinds of short cuts that stall horse-riders. The roller-skater or skate-board jockey needs a metalled surface, the skater, the skier and the canoeist need water (hard, powdered or liquid) and motorised travellers are isolated by vibration and noise.

The pedestrian shares the cyclist's go anywhere potential but does not move quickly enough to reveal the bigger picture where ranges of hills and river systems become clear. Cycle travel combines the stroller's ability to see, smell and speak to their surroundings, with the potential to cover ground five times more easily. And you get somewhere to hang luggage.

Get Lost

The relative ease of bike travel allows a more cavalier attitude to exploration. 'What's over that hill?' 'Where's this track lead?' 'What's beyond that horizon?' are questions that the two-wheeled traveller is more likely to check given their ability to glide. These rides aim to cultivate that urge.

Doorstep Tourism

Millions of international travellers take trouble to visit London and its environs. Living in or around it we have the chance to explore its detail and pursue the patterns that generations of human activity and organisation have etched on its various 'scapes. Following them we discover the village patterns of the past and understand the land use patterns of the present both of which may help us to control the future.

Go Gently

By the time you have ridden all these routes you will have improved your endurance and your riding skills, you will have brushed up your bike washing routine and your puncture drill, you will be able to set off across the wilds of Patagonia with a little confidence. It is not however, the intention of this book to turn 'unimproved' corridors into an outdoor gymnasium.

Use these rides for training if you must but concentrate on economy of effort and floating across, over and through the obstacles you encounter. A constant steady rhythm will take you further than a high maximum velocity.

If you are trying to develop raw speed find a quiet motor-road and get a heart-rate monitor. If you want to perfect rapid downhill progress or jumping obstacles you are better off finding a piece of local derelict land where these skills can be honed in safety without restricting the amenities of others; or why not enter an event on the burgeoning off-road race calendar?

Access

Some of these routes are public rights of way, others are permissive (i.e. the owners consent to allow cycle-traffic to pass). This book is not subtitled 'adventures with a bicycle' by accident. There are sections on some routes where riding is unwise, forbidden or just impossible. In some places signs make it obvious that cycle riding is not allowed. In others it is less clear, they may be marked on the OS map as footpaths but covered in tyre tracks. In some places where the rules are unclear I have avoided asking the relevant authorities for fear of prompting a redefinition of a prohibition that has in practice lapsed.

Conflict
On a wet Wednesday in winter, on some of the remoter rides you may not meet another soul for hours, on some of the pretty sections on a summer Sunday you may have to abandon any hope of riding because pedestrian traffic is too dense. Let your speed and style fit the conditions.

The rule on bridleways, where it is legal to cycle unless otherwise indicated, is that bikes must give way to pedestrians and horse riders. This rule should apply to any off-road bike riding on shared paths. Should you choose to ride in defiance of bylaws or where your status is unclear, courtesy and consideration are the best defence against persecution or even prosecution. If you ride recklessly you may escape censure but are inviting bans which will hit those who follow.

Avoid endangering others. Avoid frightening them, and their animals. Don't sneak up on people from behind - preferably rattle your brake levers, clear your throat or better still say 'hello'. Always greet people on horses with some vocal pleasantry so their beasts know you are human(ish).

On the road cyclists suffer more than anyone from the convention that travellers who wield most power should be deferred to. We should be trying to reverse this tyranny, that dominates so much of our public space, not extending it to places where quietness and humanity persist. If people give way to you always thank them.

Erosion

The other justification for bike bans is that mountain bikes shred the landscape. Minimise your impact, even if it means going through a muddy wallow rather than riding on a dry verge, and avoid skids. Taking care not to damage delicate vegetation (in late spring and summer on some less travelled routes damaging vegetation of the slashing and stinging variety is justified self-defence and public service) and soil structure should be a priority for any rambler with a bike. If, while exploring, you inadvertently stray onto private land, showing a consideration for it is your best defence against persecution.

Clothing and Equipment

Off-road cycling is a recent concept but not a recent activity. In the past there were just good and bad roads. Even in summer unmade tracks can be muddy or flooded so footwear is crucial. Waterproof cycling shoes or shoe-liners, purpose made cycle-trekking boots or lightweight fell-boots will help you to keep going.

A light bike is preferred mostly because it is more comfortable to lift and carry going up (or down) steep or stepped sections or when the going gets gluey. Conditions that prevent you from riding will also make it hard to push your bike. Sticky mud especially when reinforced with leaves or grass can soon lock wheels solid. Wide clearance between the frame and wheels, even if means sacrificing tyre tread, can save a lot of stress.

Maps

A map is a handy tool. The OS Landranger maps are quoted in the routes because their scale and detail are ideal for the rambling cyclist. The sketch maps in this book might be sufficient on their own if you are familiar with the area concerned. Bear in mind that they are not designed to be the definitive guide to the route. When cycling off-road you frequently need to use your own navigational skills. I suggest you mark the route on an OS map before setting off. This will provide maximum detail in terms of route finding and will allow diversions and alternatives to be explored in full confidence.

Bikes on Trains

Like most other things to do with our railway system - as the great experiment of privatisation looms - bikes on trains is a tricky subject. Check beforehand whether you can get on a train. Bus substitution is rampant on Sundays. In an emergency briskly board a quiet part of the train and try to bluff it out. Nerve-wracking but often effective. The regulations grow so complex that train crews may be uncertain of the status of cycle traffic.

Blatant Bias

Some readers will use cars to get to and from these rides.

In a naked attempt to discourage this no car-parking information is provided. Try and fill all your seats (or even better hire a minibus). If your passengers are qualified to drive you can make them work too and only have to stay sober one trip in five. If you join a rescue service make it the E.T.A. not a road-lobby organisation.

Before You Go

✘ familiarise yourself with the proposed route

✘ allow sufficient time and don't overestimate your ability and fitness

✘ identify refreshment stops and places to see

✘ tell someone where you are going and when you expect to return

✘ check your bike: brakes, tyres, chain, gears and riding position

What to Take

✘ waterproof and warm clothing, plus enough space to store them

✘ spare inner tubes and a puncture repair kit

✘ tyre levers and tools to remove wheels if they are not quick release

✘ a small tool kit, a pump, working lights and a bicycle lock

✘ a small first aid kit, lip-salve and water resistant sun block

✘ a map, a compass, money, food & drink

On and Off the Road

✗ ride confidently and responsibly

✗ stay alert on country lanes - you may be crossing much busier roads

✗ know your Rights of Way, if in doubt find out

✗ bridleways are generally open to cyclists. If local bylaws prohibit cycling this should be signposted

✗ always give way to horses and walkers

✗ designated cycle paths should be waymarked with a sign showing a bicycle symbol

✗ cycling is not permitted on pavements, public footpaths and open land

✗ behave responsibly and courteously, do nothing to erode hard-won access rights

✗ consider wearing a helmet when cycling off-road

✗ when cycling in a group, do not bunch and respect other road users

✗ respect and protect wildlife, plants, trees and the environment

✗ use gates (fasten behind you) and stiles to cross fences, hedges and walls

✗ do not stray from rights of way across farmland

✗ take your litter home and guard against fire

✗ make no unnecessary noise

ADVENTURES REFERENCE TABLE

No	ADVENTURE	START	FINISH	TOTAL KM	OFF ROAD	PAGE
1	GREENSAND	SEVENOAKS	SEVENOAKS	41	23	21
2	SOUTH EAST THRO' SUBURBS	GREENWICH	CHISLEHURST	14	6	30
3	INTO KENT	CHISLEHURST	PENSHURST	35	9	35
4	SOUTH TO GODSTONE	HERNE HILL	GODSTONE	35	12	42
5	STANE STREET	MERTON ABBEY	EPSOM	34	17	50
6	BOXHILL - LEITH HILL	WESTHUMBLE	WESTHUMBLE	32	25	58
7	WINDING WEY	BYFLEET	GODALMING	27	26	65
8	THE HOG'S BACK	GUILDFORD	ALDERSHOT	17	12	74
9	CUT INTO HAMPSHIRE	WEYBRIDGE	ALDERSHOT	35	31	80
10	THE GRAND JUNCTION	PADDINGTON	KINGS LANGLEY	53	51	88

ADVENTURES REFERENCE TABLE

11	INTO THE CHILTERNS	HAREFIELD	HUNTON BRIDGE	22	14	96
12	TWO WATERS	KINGS LANGLEY	TRING	19	18	102
13	ASHRIDGE & IVINGHOE	BERKHAMSTED	TRING	25	5	108
14	BARNET TO ST ALBANS	HAMP' HEATH	ST ALBANS	37	16	115
15	THE LOST LINK	HERTFORD	ST ALBANS	25	18	123
16	WILDWOODS ABOVE THE LEE	BROXBOURNE	HERTFORD	12	7	131
17	NEW RIVER & ERMINE STREET	FINSBURY PARK	WARE	35	12	137
18	KINGS CROSS TO WALTHAM	ISLINGTON	WALTHAM ABBEY	53	38	147
19	HERTS 'N' ESSEX	STANSTED ST MARGARETS	STANSTED MOUNTFITCHET	24	18	157
20	THE PEDDARS WAY	BRANDON	NORFOLK COAST	84	43	165

ADVENTURES LOCATION MAP
SOUTH OF LONDON

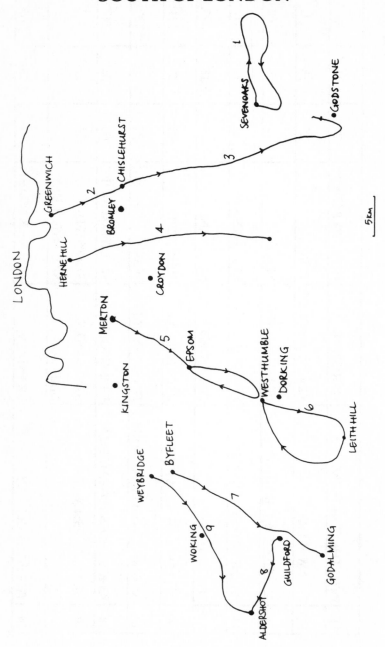

ADVENTURES LOCATION MAP
NORTH OF LONDON

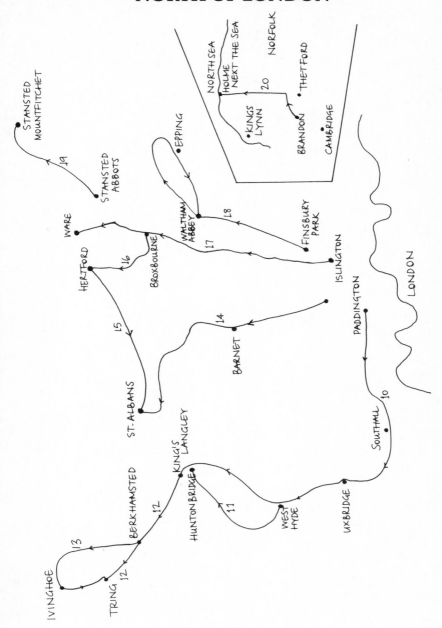

1 GREENSAND
Sevenoaks to One Tree Hill

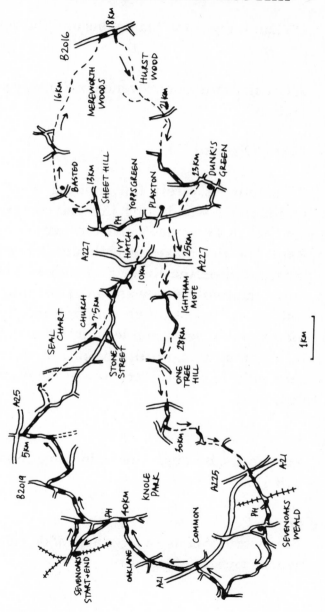

1 GREENSAND
Sevenoaks to One Tree Hill

Maps   OS Landranger 188 Maidstone and the Weald of Kent.

From   A circular tour from Sevenoaks Railway Station.

Distance 41km. Off-road 23km.

Route   This route is rarely flat running west from Sevenoaks through the woods, orchards and commons of the Greensand Ridge. Long views give the breathless rider regular reward. This ride makes several interchanges with Breathing Spaces Greensand Ridge East Ride so you can mix and match the two if you want an easier tour. Lots of hard climbing and some rough - though mostly well drained - paths and at least one technical descent. The steep terrain demands careful navigation. A wrong turning, and resulting unnecessary loss of height can be cause for tears.

Railway Access
        Sevenoaks, Borough Green. Information 071 928 5100.

Places of Interest
        Mereworth Woods - a large area of dense mixed woods and rough country.

Ightham Mote - a Medieval manor house.

One Tree Hill - view point and woods.

Knowle Park, Sevenoaks - a Tudor palace and deer park.

Food and Drink
Snax Cafe, Sevenoaks.

The Golden Hop PH, Yopps Green.

Beech Tree Restaurant, Merewith.

The Windmill PH, Sevenoaks Weald.

Sevenoaks Tea Room, Sevenoaks.

Sevenoaks Station stands close to the northern portal of a tunnel which carries the tracks from London to Hastings under the Greensand Ridge. The historic centre of the town is on top of the ridge 50 metres higher.

Turn right out of the station then fork left up St Botolphs Hill. Turn right up the High Street and left passed the Cricket Ground down Seal Hollow. (Snax Cafe is on the corner of High Street and Pembroke Road a little higher up). Turn right up Blackhall Lane and left down Parkfield. Turn left at the 'T' at the foot of Parkfield then first right into Grove Road **(5km)**. Just before the Oak Bank School entrance turn left up the public bridleway. When this path meets a tarmac road turn right then fork left onto the rising bridleway that climbs Seal Chart. Continue ahead across the sunken lane.

As the path levels off among stunted oaks and beeches the winter traveller is rewarded by unobstructed views back across Knowle Park to Sevenoaks. In summer the leaf cover allows only brief glimpses.

After St Laurences Church **(7.5km)** the path continues but is closed to cycle-traffic. Continue on foot (the path goes steeply down) or turn right to Stone Street and turn left. Keep to the left down Stone Street Road where the path down from the Church rejoins. Turn right onto Coach Road then left onto High Cross Road. The High Cross **(10km)** at the end of this road is now a road 'T'. Take the fourth arm, a bridleway straight ahead through the gate.

If you want to shorten the route turn right down the hill at High Cross and rejoin at the bridleway just below the gates to Fairlawne. The Golding Hop PH at the bottom of Sheets Hill has a garden, a pleasant aspect and serves food.

At the bottom of the hill turn left through the orchards. At Yopps Green turn left on the road which becomes the steep descent of Sheets Hill. Turn right into Crowhurst Lane and right again to descend to the river bridge **(13km)**. Turn left along the waterside track and emerging by the industrial complex at Brasted turn right up the bridleway between the factory buildings. Pass a disused sewage processing tank marked by four conifers and then turn left up a steep hill through woods turn right at the top and follow the fields edge to reach the road. Turn right then left at the Kingshill Riding School then fork right onto a bridleway past an over-grown wooden gate.

Kent is the most wooded county in Britain. Demand for poles in the hop gardens encouraged careful management of woodlands. Mereworth woods is an extensive area of mixed forest used for military training as well as forestry. It offers good off-road riding opportunities but stick to the public bridleways.

On reaching tarmac turn right. Pass the Invicta timber **(16km)** works and go straight on into the woods. After crossing a cleared area turn left then right and follow the route marked with blue flashes on the trees. At the next junction turn right then at the triangular junction a few metres further on turn left on a well surfaced forest road. Descend to a T junction and turn left. The road bears round to the right. When you come to the sign 'Horses Crossing', turn left on the blue-flash bridleway. Go straight ahead through a car-park onto a rough track through bracken and birch. Use the gate **(18km)** through the chain link fence onto the B2016. Turn right.

The big red sign on the chainlink fence 'warning security dogs are operating' - I have never seen any - is much more prominent than the concrete pillar marking the Public Right of Way hidden in the bracken. Very cheeky. The Beech Restaurant has a set-lunch menu in the French style, a good sign if you fancy a fairly extravagant feed. The second crossing of Mereworth Woods gives long views to the south east across the Medway Valley.

Turn right onto the bridleway by the telephone next to the Beech Tree Restaurant. The path diverts to the left round some mysterious metal silos so follow the perimeter and fork right to hold your original line. When the track splits into three take the central one. Turn left at the T junction slightly uphill past an aged beech tree with exposed roots (a right will take you round for another circuit of the woods). At the lone pine tree go straight on onto a loose black stone surface. Cross the perimeter road then down the steepening hill past the log barrier to cross the lane (**21km**) into a bridleway.

A marvellous prospect opens here. On a hazy evening the multiple, tree-lined horizons give the impression of an unbroken forest, the original wealden landscape. In the distance is the square tower of Shipbourne (pronounced 'Shibern') Church. The elegant brick dome in front of Allens Farm covers a well.

When the old lane forks above a newly planted apple orchard take the right leg along the fence then down the steep overgrown track. At the bottom of the track turn left into Allens Lane. Descend to cross the Bourne. Turn left through Dunks Green. The bridleway to the right marked on 1992 OS maps no longer exists so a short section of footpath must be traversed. Turn right (**23km**) just before Two View Cottages, on past the asbestos garage and left on the narrow path between fences. Climb a stile to the edge of the field and strike out on the bridlepath diagonally to the right. At the wooden gate on the other side of the field turn left to follow the fields perimeter on a tractor road. Emerge onto a lane and turn right.

If this field is planted with rape as it was in the Summer of 1994 you will find the crossing hard work. The strong fronds of the plant which is growing across the path wind themselves around your pedals making progress impossible. Send the strongest rider in your party to the front to break the trail. Or make a detour via Dunks Green (follow the signs for Planxtol.)

Go through the gate on the left and up the grand avenue of trees. At the top of the avenue bear slightly down to the left heading for the complex of gates. Go through and follow the sheep walk - marked with a single vertical yellow stake - across the lawn then drop to another gate. Go down onto a drive and left between ornamental lakes. Turn right up the path opposite the wooden bridge leading to the pagoda. On reaching the A227 **(25km)** turn right with care. The motor-traffic goes fast and a dip in the road makes this a blind spot for vehicles coming uphill. Ride up the hill and turn left over the style placed discreetly in the hedge. If you get to the main gates of Fairlawne you have overshot it.

Fairlawne was was built in the 18th Century for the minor courtier Lord Barnard. It was heavily modified in the 1840's and is now a private residence whose present owners have gone to considerable trouble to restore the house and grounds. Local gossip has it that they went so far as to offer the Local Authority three million pounds to reroute the A227 a few hundred metres to the West - still on their land - so it would not be so near the house. The Council declined. Ightham Mote hidden in the hollow is the most complete small medieval manor house in the country according to the architectural historian Pevsner, who adds that the setting is also perfect. Ightham is open to the public.

The first section of this path is again classified as a footpath (hence the stile) but by the time it goes onto National Trust land above the newly restored Ightham Mote it is once again ridable. Turn right on the road and left onto the farm road at Mote Farm. In front of the oast houses turn right up the hill. When the footpath and bridleway diverge take the bridleway up to the right. This path goes down into scrubby woodland before starting the final steep ascent of Wilmot Hill. When you come to end of the woods on top of the hill turn right on the path. On reaching the roadway opposite the old surveyors stone 'SSL 1867' **(28km)** turn left then right onto the bridleway at the finger post. As this path comes to One Tree Hill keep to the timber rails that appear on the left and come out onto the road near the T junction. Go ahead following the sign 'Riverhill 1.5 miles'. Turn left onto a bridleway **(30km)** past Orchard and Rowan Tree cottages (this turn is easily missed - it comes about 200 metres before the junction with St. Julians Road) to descend a steep and sunken track. At Kettleshill Farm turn left passed the restored Oast Houses 18th Century oast houses.

Tree roots and exposed rocks make this a technical descent but regular boggy sections where horse traffic has left deep mud allow you to check your speed.

When this road swings right turn left down the track next to the artificial lake. This lane ends on London Road **(32.5km)**. Turn left for a few metres then walk across to get into the opposite carriageway. Go round the big roundabout taking the exit signposted 'Weald'. Go straight on into Sevenoaks Weald and by the village green just passed the Windmill PH turn right into the bridleway Wickhurst Road.

Knowle House, mostly dating from the 1540's is the largest private house in England with 365 staircases and 1100 rooms. The tea rooms on the right as you enter Sevenoaks are open on Sundays.

At Wickhurst Manor turn right up the tarmaced hill, shaded in summer but very steep. Turn right on rejoining the public road (37km) and keep climbing to merge with White House Road. Go ahead to cross the Sevenoaks bypass on a high bridge then turn left into Oak Lane. Oak Lane makes a luxurious descent towards Sevenoaks finishing with a final short climb to save further brake wear. At the T junction **(40km)** turn left run passed the entrance to Knowle Park. In front of the Midland Bank fork left down the old A21 to drop to the station. Which comes after the Railway and Bicycle PH **(41.km)**.

2 SOUTH EAST THROUGH THE SUBURBS

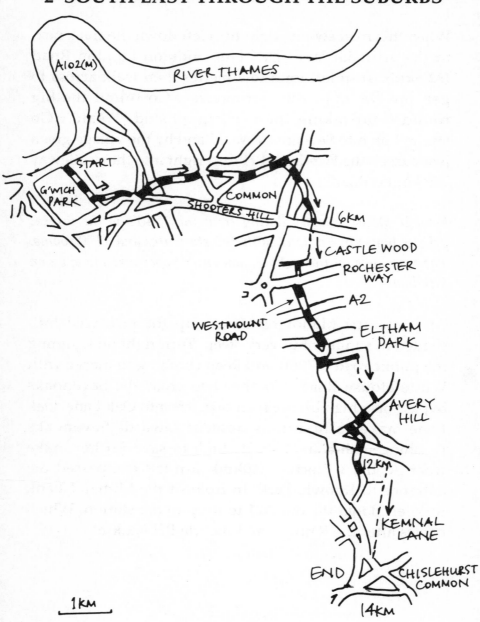

2 SOUTH EAST THROUGH THE SUBURBS

Maps   OS Landranger 177 East London.

From   Greenwich Park.

To   Chislehurst.

Distance 14km. Off-road 6km.

Route   Undemanding off-road and quiet residential back streets highlighted by bizarre buildings and a "rural" setting to finish. Climbs from the river and on Shooters Hill but otherwise level.

Railway Access
        Greenwich & Chislehurst Stations.

Places of Interest
        Greenwich.

        The Rotunda - Repository Road, Woolwich Common.

        Castle Wood and Oxleas Wood - off Shooters Hill.

        Chislehurst Common and Caves - Chislehurst.

Food and Drink
        Untold cafes in Greenwich.

Cafes in Chislehurst High Street, north east of the Common.

Pubs on Chislehurst Common.

London is a city of villages. Greenwich stands out among them as retaining a clear sense of place. It occupies a short stretch of Thames bank boundaried to the west by Deptford Creek, to the east by the grand buildings of the Naval College and Maritime Museum and to the south by the heights of Blackheath and Greenwich Park. It has loads of places to eat, a busy market, a theatre and BR trains from Charing Cross. The river bus does not unfortunately carry bikes.

From Greenwich (interchange Breathing Spaces West End to Docklands Ride) use Maze Hill or walk up through the Park to find its South Eastern exit. Follow Vanburgh Park, then turn left into Charlton Road. Fork right into Canberra Road. Then follow Charlton Park Lane across the common.

On your left you pass the Jacobean Mansion of Charlton House at present used as a library. Woolwich Common is dominated by military buildings. From the docks below troops embarked to conquer large portions of the globe. Students of militaria or architecture may like to detour left down Repository Road to visit the Artillery Museum. This eclectic collection of death and destruction machines is housed in the Rotunda, a bizarre metal-structure modelled on a military tent originally erected in the Mall to house a Waterloo victory banquet

Bear right onto Circular Way, cross into Woolwich Common Lane and continue up the steepening grade of Red Lion Lane and left into Constitution Rise. Cross Shooters Hill and enter Castle Wood **(6km)**.

Dead-straight Shooters Hill is the old Dover road, Watling Street, the High Street of London and England. If you want a direct route into or out of the Metropolis in the direction of Canterbury, Dover, Paris and Rome ease of navigation and historical interest make this a first choice.

Follow the drive into Castle Woods to find the tower. Descend to the left through the park to emerge at Crookston Road.

The Peculiar triangular structure of Severndroog Castle was built to commemorate the destruction, in 1755, of the Island fortress of Severndroog off the Malabar Coast 74° East of Greenwich. From here you can see south across London to the North Downs. Immediately to the east of Castle Wood is Oxleas Wood, a arger fragment of ancient forest saved, in 1993, from destruction (for motorway construction) by the threat of popular resistance. A shady place for a summer stop.

Turn right on Crookston Road and then left into Westmount. Follow this to Eltham High Street, turn left then right into Southend Crescent. Where the crescent joins foots Cray Road take the lane marked Charlton Park Rugby Club. Follow it into the parkland until you come to a cross-path marked with a "Green Chain" signpost (often scrambled by vandals to give wrong directions).

Turn right and follow the hedge down across the meadow. The path improves then emerges into Sparrows Lane. Turn right into Avery Hill, cross Foots Cray Road into Southwood Road. Turn left into Gerdan Road then right into Thaxted Road. Use the Footbridge **(12km)** to cross into Domonic Drive. Turn left into Molescroft and Imperial Way then left onto a narrow - and in Summer - overgrown footpath. After 100 metres this path crosses Kemnal Road, an unmade lane, turn right and follow its rural calm all the way to Chislehurst Common **(14km)**.

Chislehurst became a railway suburb in the 19th Century but retains large areas of its wooded common. Chislehurst Caves - actually an extensive chalk-mine dating back to Roman times - are open to visitors from 10.00am until 4.30 in Summer and can be reached by descending Old Hill from the Eastern end of the Common. The surviving village cockpit - on the common just north west of the junction of Common and Bromley Roads - is a rarity. Cockfighting was prohibited in 1834. Trains run to Victoria and London Bridge. There are a range of cafes on the High Street.

3 INTO KENT

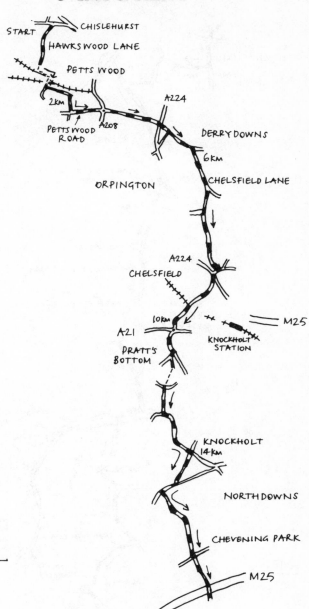

3 INTO KENT

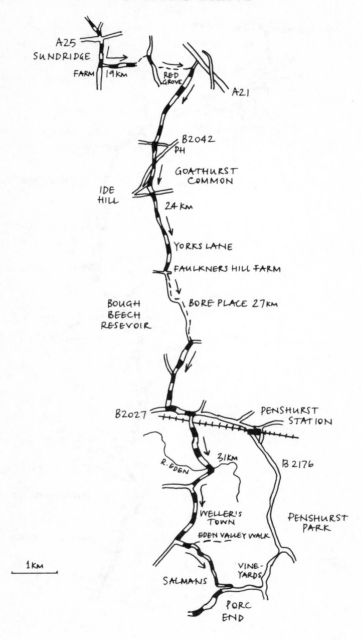

A25
SUNDRIDGE
FARM   19KM

RED
GROVE

A21

B2042
PH

GOATHURST
COMMON

IDE
HILL

24 KM

YORKS LANE

FAULKNERS HILL FARM

BOUGH
BEECH
RESEVOIR

BORE PLACE 27KM

B2027

PENSHURST
STATION

B2176

R. EDEN   31KM

PENSHURST
PARK

WELLER'S
TOWN

EDEN VALLEY WALK

VINE-
YARDS

1KM

SALMANS

PORC
END

3 INTO KENT

Maps   OS Landranger 177 East London, 188
Maidstone and the Weald of Kent.

From   Chislehurst Common.

To   Penshurst Off Road Club, Penshurst, Kent.

Distance 35km. Off-road 9km.

Route   This route entails a good deal of riding on
minor roads which once beyond Bromley are pleasant
lanes. The off-road is all rideable (with the exception of a
short footpath near the start) and the Bore Place section
is particularly pleasant. As with any route into or through
Kent - lots of hills.

Places of Interest
           Chislehurst Common and Caves.

           Petts Wood.

           PORC - Penshurst Off-Road Club, in woodland.

           Penshurst Place - Medieval Tudor house and
           gardens.

Food and Drink
           Cafes - Chislehurst.

           The Woodman PH, Goathurst Common.

From Chislehurst Common take Hawkswood Lane which begins by the Tiger's Head pub. This degenerates into the dirt-track Botany Bay Lane and drops to cross farm land in the valley of Kyd Brook. Turn left to follow the railway (this is a footpath not a bridleway) cross the tracks on the brick and metal bridge, then the timber one to emerge past the electricity sub-station into Little Thrift. Turn Left then left again into Hazelmere Road **(2km)**.

A left turn off Hazelmere Road will take you back under the railway into Petts Wood where the bridleways are not open to bikes but which makes a pleasant stop. The Petts were a Family of shipbuilders who leased the wood as a source of timber in the 16th Century. It was acquired by the National Trust in 1928 as the houses between here and the River Cray were being built.

Turn right into Crossway and left into Petts Wood Road. Over the roundabout this becomes Poverest Road and descends to cross, first a 20th century motor-route (Cray Avenue then the river Cray then the Old High Street of St. Mary Cray. Our route is briefly called Kent Road before resorting to the more modest destination tag of Chelsfield Road, fork right onto Chelsfield Lane **(6km)** which climbs slowly out of the valley towards the Kentish border.

On reaching Chelsfield turn right at the T on to Church Road which takes you across the Orpington By-pass and down Chelsfield Hill. A dual-use crossing gets you over the Sevenoaks Road **(10km)** into Rushmore Hill leading into the village of Pratts Bottom. Fork right at the village green then left onto the bridleway to the right of the

Village Hall. This climbs through houses and trees then emerges to cross open pasture. At the crossroads follow your line onto Fairtrough Road. At the T turn left into Perrys Lane to briefly follow the border of Kent and Greater London. The lane switch-backs through woods still climbing. At the next crossroads turn right into Blueberry Lane which merges into Knockholt Road **(14km)**.

You have reached the top of the North Downs and must descend into the flat bottomed Darent Valley before climbing the Greensand Ridge, the last barrier before the Weald of Kent. The first crossroads on Sundridge lane is the Pilgrims Way, a more discreet highway then either the M25 or the A24. At the time of writing the M25 is due for widening, and widening, and widening . . . .

Turn left onto Sundridge Lane which follows the perimeter of the Chevening Park Estate, at first flat and then dropping off the Downs. When the road turns left go straight onto the dirt road which passes Combe Bank School then merges with the B221 to cross the river Darent. Go over the busy A25 and continue up Church Road then left **(19km)** onto the bridleway that begins on the red-brick drive of Sundridge Place Farm. Passed Dryhill Lodge turn right uphill at the T junction onto a lane which becomes a farm track, then left through the self closing gate onto the single-track bridleway. Descend past the wood known as the Red Grove and turn sharp right onto Back Lane. This road climbs unrelenting but not too steep through woods to an asymmetric crossroads on the false flat of Mackerel's Plain. Follow the road right then turn left at the triangular green to carry on climbing. Go straight across the B2042 Ide Hill Road into Nightingale Lane (a left here takes you to the Woodman Pub - a huge establishment that serves food). Nightingale Lane crosses the fringe of Goathurst Common and emerges onto the top of the Greensand Ridge **(24km)**.

From Goathurst Common there are long views south across the wet and wooded Weald. The pattern of settlement in Kent is old small-holdings, with typically a house every few hundred metres rather than villages with empty land between. Most of the lanes have been macadamised and bridleways are a rarity. Continuous stretches of dirt riding are therefore uncommon.

Go straight ahead into Yorks Lane, a steep and deep-cut descent that should be treated with caution. At Faulkners Hill Farm where the road bends right turn left and fork immediately right onto an unmade lane which winds through remote country to Bore Place **(27km)**. Here a left-right dog-leg takes you through the assembly of old and new buildings.

Bore Place houses a dairy farm, ornamental brickworks and an educational centre. It has a Field-Trail open to the public (more information on 0732 463255).

On reaching tarmac turn right, (interchange with Breathing Spaces Greensand Ridge West Ride) then left onto the B2027 and first right over the railway. Cross the river Eden **(31km)** and turn left by the cluster of conical oast-houses. Past the Hamlet of Weller's Town go left through the broken gate on the bridleway marked by a finger post cutting the corner of a field to join a farm road. Turn left onto this then keep right by the buildings to descend past an artificial lake to Salmans. A short muddy section round the perimeter of the garden brings you to another dirt track which climbs back to tarmac. Turn right to climb to the entrance of Viceroy's Wood (PORC - Penshurst Off Road Club) **(35km)** or left past the vineyards and left again for Penshurst village and Penshurst Place.

Viceroys Wood was planted on steep ground in the 19th Century by a returned Imperialist to show the people of Kent what the foothills of the Himalayas looked like. It was neglected for forty years and the rhododendrons ran wild, but is now being restored, mostly by volunteer labour, for use as a purpose-built Mountain bike Circuit with tracks for cross-country and downhill racing and observed trials. It has a busy programme of races and events for more information ring its enthusiastic proprietor Mike Westphal on 0892 870136.

Penshurst House is mostly 650 years old though parts of it date from the 14th Century. Within easy reach of London (even in pre-bicycle days) its visitors-book is a roll-call of political and literary history. From the Black Prince to Ben Johnson. There is a local campaign to get the owners to allow cycle-traffic on a concrete trackway through the grounds at present classified as a footpath, which would give a quiet route all the way into Tonbridge.

4 GOING SOUTH TO GODSTONE

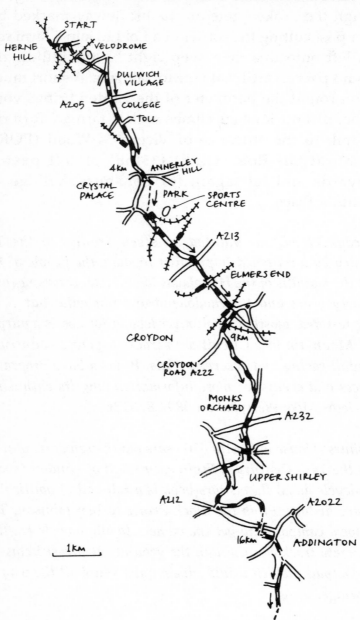

4 GOING SOUTH TO GODSTONE

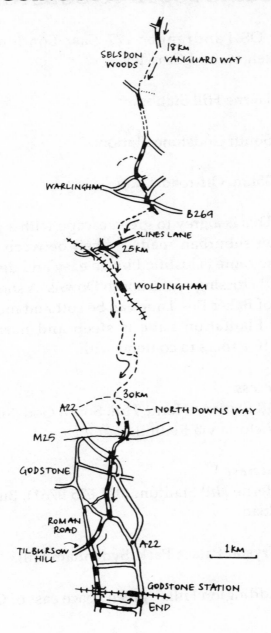

4 GOING SOUTH TO GODSTONE

Maps   OS Landranger 177 East London and 187 Dorking, Reigate and Crawley.

From   Herne Hill Station.

To   South Godstone Station.

Distance 35km. Off-road 12km.

Route   This is a grey to green escape with a good deal of riding on suburban roads - albeit between places of interest. The route is justified by an easy and delightfully unimproved crossing of the South Downs. A short section at the foot of Baker Boy Lane can be soft and muddy. The descent of Plantation Lane is steep and narrow with stones and tree roots to contend with.

Railway Access
> BR Stations Herne Hill. South Godstone from Victoria via Redhill.

Places of Interest
> Herne Hill Stadium (071 635 9761), Burbage Road.

> Crystal Palace Park, Sydenham Hill.

> Addington Hills - green space east of Croydon.

Godstone - a Surrey town that stopped growing.

Food and Drink
Cafe - Dulwich Park, off College Road.

Cafes and Pubs, Godstone.

From Herne Hill Station turn up Halfmoon Lane and right into Burbage Road. The unprepossessing entry to Herne Hill stadium is found on the left. At the end of the Burbage Road cross the roundabout and go uphill on Dulwich College Road (straight on brings you into Dulwich Park with cafe and cycle-path).

Herne Hill Stadium is London's last surviving velodrome and was resurfaced in 1993. On occasional Sundays and Monday evenings from Easter to September it hosts bicycle track-racing, a spectacle that once rivalled the popularity of Association Football. It has a licensed bar for spectators and is the home of London Recumbents who hire and sell HPV's (funny bikes).

Climb smugly past the Toll Gate (bikes no charge) At the top of the hill **(4km)** turn left then right into Westwood Hill. Enter Crystal Palace Park by the Fisherman's Gate on the right. Descend to the perimeter road and turn left. Follow this road to the top of the Grand Avenue. Turn left and follow the avenue down past the cafe to exit onto Thicket Road. At the end turn left onto Annerley Road.

On your left as you enter the park are the foundations of The

Crystal Palace, a giant conservatory of iron and glass, erected in Hyde Park for the Empire Exhibition of 1851. The Show attracted six million visitors and when it closed the venue was dismantled and taken, in numbered sections, by rail to Sydenham Hill, the dominant landmark of South London.

For eighty years the Palace stood at the centre of an early leisure-centre where music, theatre and fireworks were regular attractions. Prior to 1924 the FA cup final was played here. The sporting tradition continues with a 12,000 seat athletics stadium and bicycle road-racing in the park on Tuesday evenings. The remains of the amusement park are boating lakes and 29 dinosaurs made of brick, iron and plaster.

Continue down Annerley Road, on into Elmers End Road and right at the T onto Croydon Road. Over the bridge turn left (**9km)** onto The Glade which becomes Orchard Avenue. Cross into Hartland Way. At the end turn right then left onto a tarmac path marked 'Pinewoods' follow the School fence with open woodland to your left. Emerge onto Sandpits Lane then turn left at the Sandrock PH **(12.5km)** to climb Upper Shirley Road which becomes Shirley Hills Road.

The Monk's Orchard Estate, a suburban paradise of the 1930's is complemented by the fancy brickwork of the brand new houses in Sandpits Lane. Dreams of rustic idylls persist. On the right of Shirley Hills Road is the entrance to Addington (or Shirley) Hills a wooded park of vertical slopes and long views which occasionally hosts races in yet more two-wheeled disciplines of mountain bike and cyclo-cross.

A left turn down Bishops Walk (the 25mph speed limit informs this is a private road) brings you to a timber barrier. Beyond it is Addington Palace and a drive leading to the A212 Gravel Hill (**16km**).

The Central section of Addington Palace dates from 1770. With grounds landscaped by Capability Brown but converted for golf a hundred years later. In the 19th Century it was the seat of the Archbishop of Canterbury. In the 20th it has served as a military hospital and country club. It is now the Royal College of Church Music. There is a notice on Gravel Hill, a dual carriageway where motor-traffic goes fast, which states 'Road Safety - always use the Footbridge'. This Orwellian pervertion of truth should of course read ' Road Danger - always use the footbridge'.

Use the footbridge and go ahead up the broad tree lined path to turn left and left again into Crossways, a residential cul-de-sac. Bear right to emerge on Selsdon Park Road. Turn right then left onto Featherbed Lane. Fork left onto Courtwood Lane.

Courtwood Lane ends in a turning circle which marks the limit of Greater London which since it has no political identity at the moment is marked by the Borough of Croydon. Into the woods and into Surrey.

At the end of Courtwood Lane (**18km**) bear right onto a bridleway (Baker Boy Lane) with Selsdon Woods on the right and fields behind a hedge on the left. The old course of Baker Boy Lane, a deep-worn rut on the right is overgrown, the current track often soft and muddy. When the old lane enters woods after a few hundred metres the going gets easier. Turn left on regaining tarmac at Farliegh Road. Go ahead into Old Farliegh Road and Sunny Bank and then right into Chelsham road left then right into High Lane, then right into Plantation Lane.

The area east and south of Chelsham and Warlingham has lots of good bridleways to explore. Warlingham has just been hit with that classic '90's planning mistake, an out-of-town superstore. At the foot of Plantation Lane the other harbinger of the middle-England low-density, life-style - the suburban golf course.

Plantation lane descends along the valley side then drops steeply to cross it and climb - through the golf club - to join Slines Lane **(25km)**. Turn right. Then go ahead to pass under the railway viaduct and make an immediate sharp left up the private road (public bridleway) into Marden Park.

This dry windgap valley is a rare chance to cross the South Downs without the bothersome noise of motor-traffic. Even the railway on the left dissappears into a tunnel.

Beyond the School buildings turn right and climb to cross the North Downs Way **(30km)**. Keep left at the crossing then fork right as the rutted track returns to public road. Descend to cross the M25 and A22 on bridges and the A25 at ground level into Church Lane. Descend to cross Gibbs Brook **(33km)** and make a right and left up the steep moss banked lane to join the roman road over Tillburstow Hill Common. Turn right* to descend into Godstone **(35km)**.

Gibbs Brook runs east to join the Medway. On the other side of Tilburstow Common water runs west into the Mole, and both rivers finally turn north to join the Thames fifty miles apart. Despite its proximity to London's physical boundry, Godstone has a strong Surrey identity. This probably has something to do with the absence of a direct rail line. (South Godstone the nearest Station has trains to London via Redhill.) The pubs and cafes round Godstone green have had their passing trade usurped by the big motor-roads that interchange nearby rather than at the village centre.

*A left turn on Tillburstow Hill leads south (turn left after the railway bridge to reach South Godstone Station) to join the A22. Follow this road, or parallel lanes to the west, to join the B2028 near New Chapel. Continue over Turners Hill to Lindfield then the B2112 at Haywards Heath to Ditchling (recently sanctified by the passing of the Tour de France), the beacon interchange with the South Downs Way and a clean escape to Brighton.

5 STANE STREET

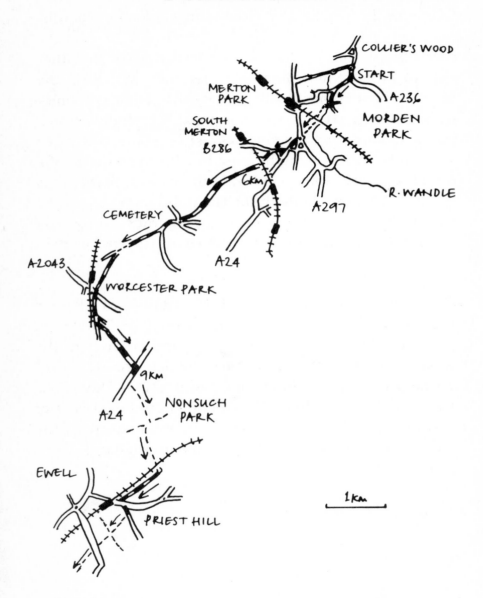

5 STANE STREET

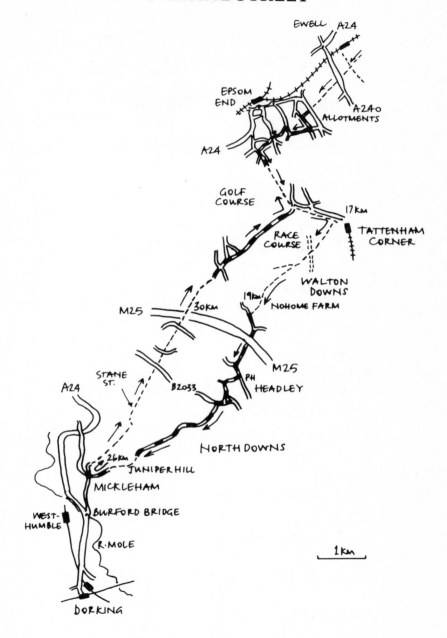

EWELL A24

EPSOM
END

A240
ALLOTMENTS

A24

GOLF
COURSE

17km

RACE
COURSE

TATTENHAM
CORNER

WALTON
DOWNS

M25 30km 19km NOHOME FARM

M25

STANE
ST.

A24 B2033 PH HEADLEY

NORTH DOWNS

26km JUNIPER HILL

MICKLEHAM

WEST-
HUMBLE BURFORD BRIDGE

R. MOLE

1 Km

DORKING

5 STANE STREET

Maps   OS Landranger 176 WestLondon and 187
Dorking, Reigate and Crawley.

From   Merton Abbey SW19, off Stane Street (A24).

To   Epsom Downs via Burford Bridge, Surrey.

Distance 34km. Off-road 17km.

Route   After an interesting if somewhat intricate trip
out of Inner London the last quarter of this ride is through
open country. The alternate endings give it a lollipop
shape. It connects with other routes in the North Downs.
Some of the final off-road sections are steep and can be
muddy.

Railway Access
          BR Stations at Clapham (follow signs A24
          Dorking to get to the start), Epsom, Boxhill and
          Dorking. Information 071 928 5100.

Places of Interest
          Morden Hall Mills, Merton.

          Nonsuch Park, Cheam.

          Epsom Downs.

          Box Hill.

Food and Drink
> Cafe, Morden Hall Park.

> Ryka's Cafe, Burford Bridge.

The A24 Stane Street is the Roman Road to Chichester, it branches from the A3, Portsmouth Road at Clapham Common and rolls south through Balham and Tooting. Its line is lost where it crosses the River Wandle, which is where our route starts.

From the Colliers Wood gyratory take the A236 Christchurch Road south and second right into Liberty Avenue; follow this into Brangwyn Crescent. Turn right onto the river bank. Cross the wooden footbridge and turn left onto the asphalt path. This is Bunce's Meadow, part of Morden Hall Park. Progress along the Wandle bank is blocked by a railway so follow the path to the right and cross the tracks by the high footbridge. Another 30 metres along the track is an entry bearing the faded message 'This gate is closed at sunset.' There is no gate. Go through into the water gardens.

The river Wandle was an important source of power until the 19th Century. Morden Hall mill ground snuff from hard tobacco. In hot weather the smell was overpowering and the workers wore paper hats and cloths over their faces. The decline in snuff snorting led to the mills closure in 1920's. At the same time the tiny village of Morden was swamped by housing estates. After a spell as a Nursing home the buildings and grounds passed to the National Trust. Among the attractions here is a waterside cafe open 10:00 -17:00.

Leave Morden Hall Park **(2km)** by the entrance to the west of the cafe and cross into Aberconway Road. Follow the Morden one-way system and take Crown Lane then Links Avenue. Go under the railway-bridge and turn left into Old Links Avenue. Follow the fenced footpath **(6km)** to the right along the edge of the neglected ILEA sports ground. As the path gets steeper the tarmac gets worse, but this won't matter because you are walking anyway (an alternative legally rideable route uses Hillcross Avenue).

Past the boarded up changing rooms the path descends through trees. The hill has taken us out of the Wandle valley, the concrete culvert at the foot of the park drains into Beverley Brook the next westward tributary of the Thames.

Straight on down the tarmac path Bow Lane then right onto Lower Morden Lane over the small roundabout and past the entry to Battersea Cemetery. As the road bears left go straight on into Green Lane. The dirt road becomes a bridle path which takes you into the LB of Sutton. Green Lane becomes a residential road and bends left to take the right side of the little watercourse. Follow it down to Worcester Park. Under the bridge to your right is Kingston, Surrey. Our route stays in Greater London for the moment crossing into Lynwood Drive with a left right dog-leg. At the triangular green fork left into Sandringham Road which becomes Tudor Avenue, right into Killester Road and left into Sparrow Farm Road which hits the A24 (Stane Street again) just as it crosses into Surrey.

Nonsuch Park was the sight of the village of Cuddington which Henry VIIIth had cleared to build an unsurpassed (hence the name) hunting retreat. The luxurious palace was constructed using stone from the dissolved Merton Priory. To ensure its high quality Henry employed master craftsmen from Italy. The house was demolished in 1682 and materials re-recycled to build Durdans House in Epsom. The present building in the park dates from the 16th Century but was extensively restyled in 1804.

Cross the road and enter Nonsuch Park **(9km)**. On your right is a car park, from there follow the path into the park. Go to the left of the house then straight on with the Aviary on your left. Turn right at the T junction then left through the hedge over an embankment to find a stony single track footpath across a patch of wild ground. The path becomes asphalt and leads to a tunnel under a railway embankment, to the right of the fenced electricity sub-station. Turn right up Holmwood Road then left onto the A232 and immediately right, sign-posted for Banstead. Take the bridle path to the right across the sports ground. Cross the A240 on the 'bridleroad'.

The OS map marks this section as bridleway but it is marked with a 'no cycling' sign. It crosses more residential roads and a faded sign threatens a £20 fine to any who dare cycle. This bears the signature of Dr. Grimes Town Clerk who sounds like Dickensian eminence got up to frighten the children.

After the allotments on the right Bridle Road becomes Bridle End so turn left **(14.5km)** up Albert Road, right into College Road, left into Lynwood Road. Turn right at the T junction into Burgh Heath Road and left up the horse path by Dell Cottage.

Dr. Grimes has another sign here. This path runs up onto Epsom Downs, a famous cockney playground. Observe the bylaws which are frequently displayed. Model aeroplanes over 5kg are prohibited.

At the golf course keep left. Cross the road and follow the path to Tattenham Corner **(17km)**. From here on you are sharing horse-paths, go slowly especially downhill and give way to those trying to control four-legged path churners.

As you see the giant grandstand rising on the right look back for a fine view. Each June the Epsom Derby is run here over 1.5 miles. It is called a flat race because it has no fences but the 'U' shaped course climbs to the this bend before descending to the finish making it the toughest test in the World for three year old horses who unlike cyclists find uphill easier than down. In the distance you can see the round steeple of Headley Church, prepare to chase it; slowly. It won't run away.

Cross the racecourse and cut the curve. Cross the far side by the big '8' (furlongs) sign. As the path forks bear right, then as you emerge from the woods go down across the gallops. Take care especially before 12:00 when the race horses are exercised. You are aiming for the wooded bridleway which runs south from the Down's perimeter track (at GR 212 571) just west of Noholme Farm **(19km)**. This muddy bridleway rejoins tarmac at North Lodge. Turn left downhill, follow the sign for Headley and pass under the M25. Turn left, signposted Headley and Boxhill, and right into Slough Lane. Ignore Langley Lane, the interesting looking bridleway climbing to the right and go left down Tumber Street. Turn right at the cross roads, resisting Crabtree Lane another tempting track then left onto Lodge Bottom Road **(22km)**. This 2.5 miles of winding lane descends to Juniper Hill on the old Dorking Road turn left for Burford Bridge (interchange Leith Hill Route and Breathing Spaces Mole Valley & Box Hill Ride). A cycle track follows the A 24 to Dorking.

The return to Epsom is via a rolling bridleway on the line of Stane Street.

Just before Lodge Bottom Lane joins the Old Dorking Road **(26km)** turn right up a steep stony track. This becomes a confusing maze of roughly parallel tracks over Mickelham Down then settles on a Roman-straight line over a series of lanes and the M25 **(30km)**. Rejoin tarmac just past Thirty Acre Barn. Go straight on into Downs Road, past Langley Vale to the Racecourse. Pass under the equine flyover **(33.5km)** and turn right to rejoin the outward route at Tattenham Corner **(34km)**.

The trip to Epsom for the Derby is a traditional Londoner's day out by foot, omnibus, railway, limousine, helicopter or bicycle. The event is run on a Wednesday in June although there is much talk of rescheduling it to Sunday.

58

6 BOXHILL-LEITH HILL-BOXHILL

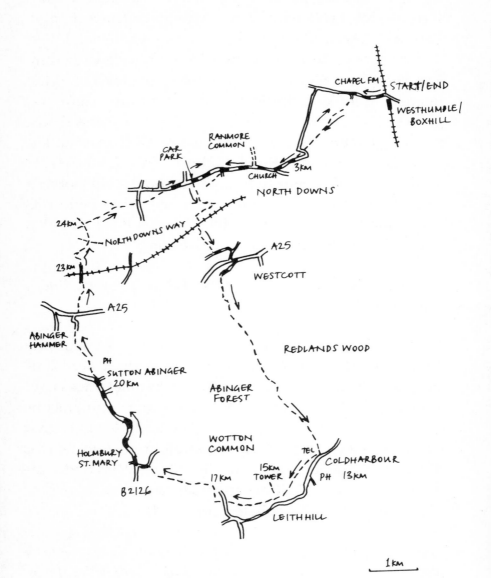

6 BOXHILL-LEITH HILL-BOXHILL

Maps   OS Landranger 187 Dorking, Reigate and Crawley.

From   A circular route from Boxhill (formerly Westhumble) BR Station.

Distance 32km. Off-road 25km.

Route   A quiet circuit through the South Downs to the highest point in south east England. Lots of climbing and some muddy tracks.

Railway Access
          Westhumble. Information 071 928 5100.

Places of Interest
          Leith Hill Tower.

Food and Drink
          The Plough PH, Coldharbour.

          Leith Hill Tower (fine weekends only).

          The Volunteer PH, Sutton Abinger.

          Ryka's Cafe, Burford Bridge is open in the evenings. Reach it by turning right out of Boxhill BR crossing the A24 and following the cycle track left to Burford Bridge

Turn left out of the Station and cross the train tracks on Chapel Lane (interchange with Breathing Spaces Mole Valley & Boxhill Ride). Turn left by the Chapel and climb a narrow tarmac drive. When the drive bares left fork right up a single track bridleway.

Looking back across the Mole Gap you can see the steep slopes of Boxhill, Juniper Hall and the winding valley known as 'Little Switzerland'.

On meeting a larger track fork right onto the uphill bridleway. This levels out among woods. When it reaches a tarmac lane go straight over remaining on the bridleway. When the path emerges onto a road turn right towards the flint church with a steeple **(3km)**. (If you would like an easier start to the ride carry straight on at Chapel Farm then take the first left to climb Ranmore Common on a tarmac lane, complete with hairpin bend. At the top of the hill turn right and rejoin the route at St. Barnabas Church.) Right at the T junction brings you onto a broad grassy ride with a motor-road running down the middle.

This is Ranmore Common (interchange with Breathing Spaces Leith Hill & The Surrey Weald Ride). A track by the first buildings on the right leads to Tanners Hatch YHA. The National Trust (Warden 0372 453 401) owns and manages most of the remaining open chalk downland in this area. Only ride on the bridleways.

On the far side on the second car-park on the left (marked

NT Ranmore Common) turn left onto a pressed cinder bridleway. This runs through woods to the top of the North Downs escarpment and then plunges steeply down towards the first of the Surrey Weald.

Erosion of the delicate chalk soil has left exposed tree roots. These form vertical steps which make the descent tricky.

After a short distance on the fall line the path bears left. Turn right at the 'T' junction at the bottom then left through the small wooden gate. The path runs between two fields then under a railway bridge. Swing right then left at the farm buildings onto a pressed rubble road past old brick built Rookery Drive. After crossing the watercourse fork left and continue above the chain of ornamental lakes. At the triangular stand of trees fork right uphill.

This is Greensand soil of the Low Weald; whereas the chalk of the downs is slippery after wet weather, a little water on this stuff packs it together and makes traction easier. The path here is clearly an old country road. Years of traffic have eroded the soil and sunk it several feet below the level of the surrounding hillside toppling trees in the process. This slow erosion by feet, hooves, cart and latterly bicycle wheels contrasts with the dramatic damage done by four-wheel drive motor-traffic on the route we join at the edge of the woods.

On emerging from the sunken lane turn left on either the track running along the edge of the field or the sunken road in the edge of the woods. The quality of this road varies considerably making an interesting run as it climbs gently then descends to Coldharbour, where it emerges opposite the Plough PH **(13km)**. Don't cross the road, unless you want refreshment. Turn right by the old style telephone box, up onto Coldharbour Common.

The Leith Hill massive is the highest part of the sandstone ridge which runs east-west, parallel to the North Downs. The area is dotted with 'highest, in south east England' superlatives, including pub - the Plough at Coldharbour, cricketfield, Coldharbour Common - sloping with short boundaries for quick scoring - and point, Leith Hill summit.

Go straight on past the cricket pitch, keep slightly left at the first big interchange then left up the sharp rise. Over the top of the hill descend crossing another path then climb to the Tower **(15km)**.

The tower on Leith Hill was built in 1766 by Richard Tull who is buried beneath its floor, supposedly to raise the level of the hilltop to 1,000 feet, and certainly to provide an impressive viewpoint. Its soft brick is carved with a fine selection of antique graffiti. The tower is open 11 till 2.30 on fine weekends and Bank Holidays. Teas are served in the ground floor room. It is said that from the top you can see into thirteen counties. Verification would demand a clear day and an atlas. Surrey, Sussex, Hampshire, Kent, Berkshire, London, Middlesex, Buckinghamshire, Oxfordshire, Wiltshire, Hertfordshire and Essex seems the most likely list. Without climbing the Tower you can see back to your right the steeple of St. Barnabas, Ranmore Common and trace the line of your descent from the

North Downs.

Descend through the carpark beyond the Tower. Go carefully as there may be walkers about even on quiet days. On reaching the road (interchange with Breathing Spaces Leith Hill & Surrey Weald Ride) cross onto the bridleway to pass the barrier of fallen trees. Turn right by the gate and yew tree. Obliquely cross two tracks, then climb winding. Turn left onto the hard farm road. Beyond the rubble tip **(17km)** the path narrows to single track and climbs into the woods.

This section starts with long views south across the Weald and once in the dense woods gives an excellent switch back ride even in the wettest riding conditions. The tarmac section that follows is the only significant road riding of the whole itinerary, all downhill through the nineteenth century village of Holmbury St Mary which feels more like the Forest of Dean than the outer suburbs.

On meeting the road turn left then right at the T to descend right through Holmbury St. Mary. Just past the left turn to the Youth Hostel turn right then left. At the T junction by the Volunteer PH **(20.5km)** turn right then after 20 metres left up a driveway. Fork right onto the single-track at the green gate. When the path opens out keep to the edge of the fence. Descend on the rutted farm track then turn left and right through the farmyard with magnificent timber and tile barn. Pass the watercress beds and recross the A25 with great care as motor-traffic speeds over the brow of the hill to the right. Take the bridleway straight ahead go through the wooden gate and across the pasture. Beyond a second wooden gate lies a triangular green, follow its left edge and find a bridlepath descending at the first corner you reach. As a farm road merges from the left go on over the railway line **(23km)** and on towards the ominous slope of the North Downs. When the path forks turn left up the hill turn right at the hairpin round the stump of an old brick structure.

When the path reaches the plateau keep straight ahead on the maze of paths until you strike the massively eroded track(s) running perpendicular **(24km)** Turn right on these and follow them across one motor road to merge with a second that takes you onto Ranmore Common for a choice of descents to West Humble **(32km)**.

7 THE WINDING WEY TO GODALMING

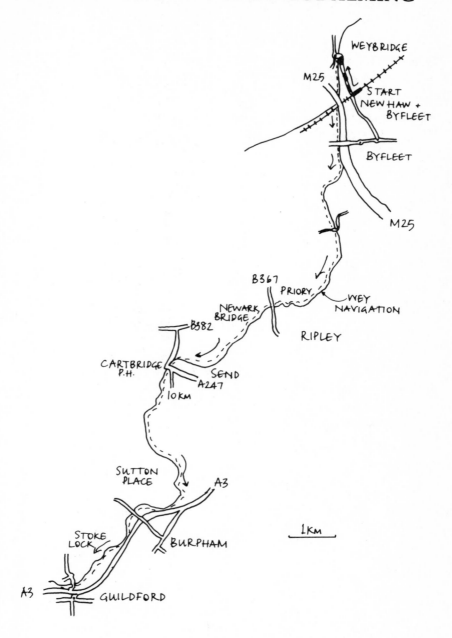

7 THE WINDING WEY TO GODALMING

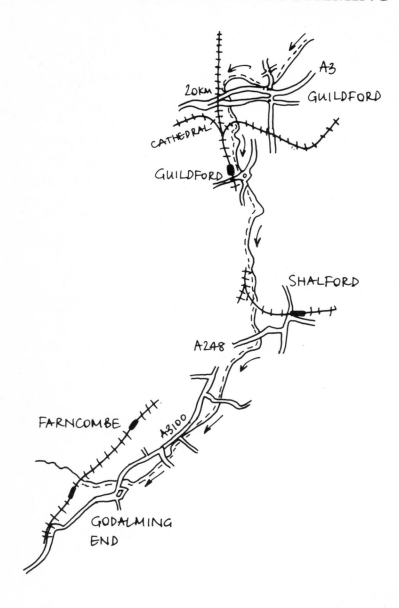

20KM

A3

GUILDFORD

CATHEDRAL

GUILDFORD

SHALFORD

A248

FARNCOMBE

A3100

GODALMING
END

1KM

7 THE WINDING WEY TO GODALMING

Maps   OS Landranger 176 West London, and 186
Aldershot and Guildford. The route passes
briefly onto 187 Dorking, Reigate and
Crawley but the whole route is easy to follow
and the third map is a luxury.

From   Byfleet, Surrey. the junction of the Wey
Navigation and Basingstoke Canal.

To   Godalming, Surrey.

Distance 27km. Off-road 26km.

Route   After a grim first mile under and beside the
M25 this ride is surprisingly rural, punctuated after wet-
weather with spectacular weirs. Entering along the river
is the best way to discover the ancient town of Guildford
and the charms of Godalming. Some sections of the path
are rough but the absence of hills, motor-traffic and
serious navigational problems make it an easy to enjoy
itinerary.

Railway Access
BR Stations New Haw and Byfleet,
Weybridge, Guildford, Godalming.
Information 071 928 5100.

Places of Interest
Newark Priory - a romantic riverside ruin.

Stoke Lock - one of the oldest pound locks in Britain.

Guildford - the County Town of Surrey.

St Catherines Hill - steep and wooded overlooking the Wey at Guildford.

Godalming - home of the Cyclists' Touring Club.

Food and Drink

The Anchor PH, Pyrford Lock.

The New Inn, Cartbridge.

The Jolly Farmer PH, Millmeads, Guildford.

By the Wey Restaurant, Farncombe.

Reach Byfleet from Weybridge using the Cut into Hampshire route or from New Haw and Byfleet BR Station by turning right onto Byfleet Road then left onto the towing path at New Haw Bridge. Where the waterways divide the Wey Navigation is the left fork going south under the railway.

Byfleet is the junction of the Wey Navigation (not a canal but an 'improved' river) and the Basingstoke Canal. The Waterloo-Portsmouth mainline crosses on Byfleet Bridge and the M25 runs on stilts overhead; bringing together four centuries of infrastructure.

At the Byfleet Boat Club go up to the bridge and turn right to the footpath that continues to the left of the boatyard gate.

From Weybridge to Pyrford the Navigation and the natural course of the Wey are on opposite sides of the flat flood-plain. The hummocks to be seen are not prehistoric burial-chambers or glacial drumlins, they are for golf. Before Walsham Lock, one of the few turf sided locks left in the country, the towing path becomes a causeway between the two water-courses. They unite at a long weir. From here straight-cut pounds alternate with winding stretches of navigable river.

Cross the weir on the concrete footbridge **(6km)**. Cross the canal at Newark Lock close to the ruins of the priory and recross it at Newark Bridge on the B367. Make sure you secure all gates through this open pasture section. The going can be tough through the cattle tracks but try not to further erode the grass by opting for an easier route.

The ruins on the right are of the 13th Century Augustinian Newark Priory. The river runs behind it. The channel to the left of the Navigation is the mill stream for Newark Mill which burned down in 1966. Only the Mill House remains. Just beyond Newark Bridge the channels are briefly reunited and boats follow a stretch of winding river. Below Papercourt Lock it trifurcates into the natural river the Navigation and a parallel drainage channel.

Cross to the west bank Papercourt Lock. At Cartbridge cross to the east bank with care on the busy A247 bridge by the New Inn **(10km)**.

Beyond Cartbridge the land on either side begins to undulate and the North Downs come into view.

After passing through two gates cross the cut on Send Church Bridge to skirt the private grounds of Sutton Place. The path is eroded in places here and requires some care. If you need to put your foot down do it on the landward side.

Richard Weston lived at Sutton Place. It was he who commissioned the first improvements to the Wey in this area between 1618 an 1620. The length from Guildford to the Thames was navigable by 1650 preceding Britain's short canal boom by at least a hundred years.

Cross the cut by the bridge at deep Bowers Lock. Cross the River to come up to the Navigation at Stoke Lock **(16km)**. At Stoke Bridge on the Woking Road cross the River Wey which is merging with the Navigation from the East.

Beyond Bowers Lock the path enters Riverside Park in the suburbs of Guildford. On Stag Hill to the left the brick-built Cathedral looks remarkably like a power station. Stoke Lock is the oldest pound lock (i.e. with two gates) in the County of Surrey. Before this technology was developed 'flash locks' consisting of a single gate beside a weir were the norm.

Traversing these was an unreliable process particularly going upstream and since they were very wasteful of water there was a limit on how frequently they could be opened. The development of canal engineering which allowed cheap bulk-carriage of iron ore and coal was a significant factor in the early onset of industrialisation in England. The amount of goods carried by one horse increased by a factor of eighty when waterborne.

With care cross the double bridge of Woodbridge Road and continue on the west bank on the road by the garage - Woodbridge Meadows. After the railway crosses on the high brick Dapdune Bridge rejoin the tow path. This is the final section of the Wey Navigation and some old wharves and warehouses, remnants of the old timber, paper and printing trades can be seen along the bank.

Climb the steps to the Walnut footbridge and turn right if you want to reach Guildford BR Station. Use the Town bridge **(20km)** to explore the historic city centre or connect with the Hog's Back Ride. If you don't fancy the steps continue to Mill Meads where there is ramped access to the towing path.

Beyond the confines of the city centre the river opens onto Millmeads a pleasant water-side park. If you have been up to town for supplies this is the place for a picnic. The Jolly Farmers PH serves food. If you are eager to shift modes of travel you can hire a boat here (tel 0483 504494). This is the Godalming Navigation which was completed in 1764 and run as a separate business from the Wey until they both came under the administration of the National Trust in 1968.

Cross to the west bank as you leave Mill Meads under the wooded flank of St Catherine's Hill. Stay on this side past the new wooden bridge - which carries the Pilgrims Way - even though the path looks sandy, eroded and unpromising.

Note the rolling post at the point of the horseshoe bend which caught the tow lines of barges to prevent their horses pulling them into the bank. As the Navigation bears left for Godalming we pass 'The Guns Mouth', on the far bank. Today it looks like a marina or boatyard but it was once the entrance to the Wey and Arun Junction Canal which once connected the Thames to the Solent via the river Arun, Arundel and Portsmouth. It was designed to give a safe route for supplies during war with France but by the time it was opened in 1816 Napoleon had been defeated. Like many of the later ambitious canals water supplies for the summit were always a problem. The Arundel/Portsmouth Canal failed and although the Wey Arun paid dividends in the 1830's it was killed off by the railways and closed in 1868. Many of the locks and reservoirs can be found dry and overgrown. A trust is slowly restoring the cut.

The last leg to Godalming is pleasant, the path stays on the West side with no further crossings the canal swings from south to south west at the Guns Mouth **(23km)**. Food is available at Farncombe Boat House. On entering Godalming cross to the east bank on the town bridge and follow the tarmac path.

Town bridge was always the limit of navigation but it is worth pressing on to visit the extensive water-side memorial to read the sad and appropriately watery story of local hero J.G. Phillips. Godalming is cute with a capital 'Q' and the monument is a good place to start exploring the well preserved town. Godalming is a genteel place but we would expect nothing less for the headquarters of the CTC.

Emerge onto the road at the Old Bridge turn left and right into Vicarage Walk. When it ends turn left up the leafy lane to find Godalming station **(27km)**.

8 ON THE HOG'S BACK

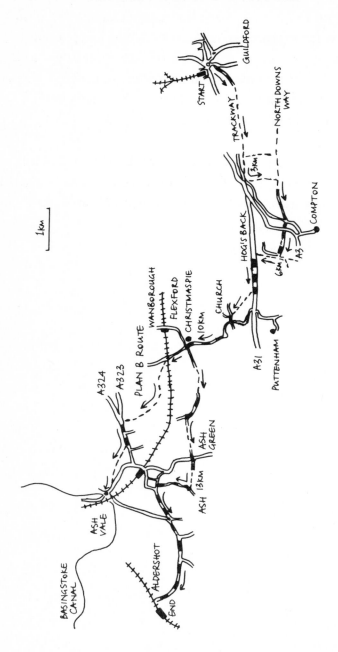

8 ON THE HOG'S BACK

Maps   OS Landranger 186 Aldershot and Guildford.

From   Guildford, Surrey.

To   Aldershot, Hampshire.

Distance 17 km. Off-road 12km.

Route   Starts on a prehistoric continuation of Guildford High Street. Wooded downland gives way to alternate endings, swampy green lanes or sandy Surrey heath. Steep climbs and slippery descents with short boggy sections close to Aldershot.

Railway Access
        BR Stations Guildford, Ash, Wanborough, Aldershot. Information 071 928 5100.

Places of Interest
        Guildford.

        Aldershot - 19th Century garrison town.

Food and Drink
        Importers Coffee House, Guidford High Street 9-5 six days per week.

        Gallery Tea Shop, Compton.

Guildford has been an important route-centre as long as humans have wandered through Southern England. In this area the parallel prehistoric tracks running along the North Downs from Wiltshire to Canterbury (named the Pilgrims Way in the 19th Century) cross the river Wey. As a strategic gap in the Downs it was fortified by the Normans and the Portsmouth Road became a classic outing for pioneer cyclists and motorists in the early 20th Century. The town centre is beset with one-way streets which obscure its historic justifications but apart from that Guildford tries hard to engage the tourist. The best place to begin an exploration of the town is the cobbled High Street which climbs steeply east from the Town Bridge. If you want details of access to the Town's antiquities and the galleries and guided walks call in at the Information Centre in the 13th Century vaulted basement of number 72 the High Street.

Emerging from Guildford Station either turn right to walk south along the Portsmouth Road to the Town Bridge or follow the gyratory system over the river on Bridge Street to find the same destination. From the bridge cross the Portsmouth Road to climb The Mount.

The Mount climbs very steeply away from Guildford straight onto the Downs. In an era of pedestrians and livestock it was the main-drag out of Town. In the conversion to wheeled vehicles it has become a quiet cul-de-sac. Walking is allowed.

The Mount emerges from buildings into a hill-top track on the spine of the Hog's Back. As the track is joined from the right by the A31 fork left into the lane running down to Compton and just past the Pillar Box at the junction turn left into a steep bridleway **(3km)**. The descent is narrow and steep - take care. At the junction with the official line of the North Downs Way turn right and continue past farm buildings to emerge at Compton. There is a gallery here with a cafe open seven days a week.

The lands south of the North Downs Way belong to the Loseley Estate, famous for ice-cream and yoghurt. This far west the chalk out-crop is narrow and we are already onto Greensand soil. This track is called Sandy Lane.

Turn right and immediately left to pass under two flyovers. Just beyond the second leave the private drive and fork left onto the path. Continue through lovely woods to a staggered cross-path **(6km)**. Turn right and climb back up to the top of the Downs.

Just below the summit of the climb - The Hog's Back again - yet another manifestation of the North Downs way crosses our track.

This is a private road. If you are coming the other way descend carefully as children from the house with the archway may be playing here. On reaching the dual carriage way turn left and follow it for around 800 metres until you reach Grey Friars Farm.

The splendid symmetry and long views north and south made the Hog's Back a popular tourist route earlier in the Century. Contemporary 'improvements' at the western end near

Farnham set to make it even more like a freeway unfit for human-scale travel.

Cross to the central reservation and ride on its verge another 30 metres further west until you are opposite the bridleway marked with a gate and finger post. Cross the eastbound carriageway and begin the descent to Wanborough Manor.

This path connects Wanborough with Compton and was once busy enough to be metalled. Vestiges of tarmac remain on the upper sections.

Turn left at St Bartholomew's Church and right on meeting Westwood Lane. At Christmaspie **(10km)** turn left into Green Lane East. (if you want to make a circuit before returning to Guildford or want to reach the Basingstoke Canal avoiding Aldershot go straight on and switch to PLAN B) Go straight on at the cross and at the triangular green turn left passed the duck pond (complete with duck kennel.)

This unimproved country road can be ill-drained after wet weather. The worst section is muddy but quite short.

The path becomes a tarmac road cross into Ash Green Lane West. Cross the disused railway **(13km)** and turn right at the T junction. At the end of this lane turn left. At the almost immeadiate T junction with Ash Church Road a right turn takes you to Ash Station (Services to Guildford and Reading), and the Basingstoke Canal at the

Ash Vale Bridge. A left turn followed by straight on at the roundabout takes you into Aldershot **(17km)** for trains to Waterloo.

PLAN B

Just beyond the railway bridge turn left through a gate onto a bridleway Follow this green lane as it bears right, passes farm buildings and the back of a housing estate before climbing to join the A323 just where the A324 joins it **(12km)**.

If you pass this way on a Wednesday evening you may see a man with a flag and a sweaty cyclist or two sweeping round the bend. This turn is part of a local time-trial course code CC123A.

Turn left on the A323 to Ash and at the Nightingale pub turn right into the sandy track Nightingale Lane. Keep to the left onto Gravel Pit Hill. The track peters out over the lightly wooded hill crest then descends behind buildings on the left to join an unmade lane which merges into Ash Hill Road by a War Memorial. Turn right down the hill, go straight over the roundabout to join the Basingstoke Canal at Ash Vale Bridge **(14km)** (joins Cut into Hampshire route) where a left turn takes into Aldershot or a right towards Woking, Byfleet, Weybridge and the Thames.

9 CUT INTO HAMPSHIRE

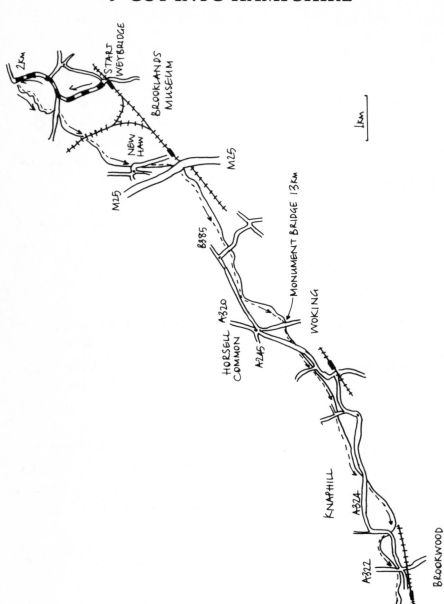

9 CUT INTO HAMPSHIRE

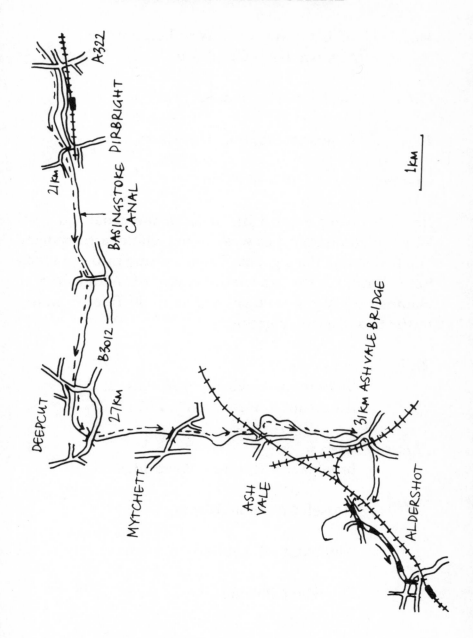

9 CUT INTO HAMPSHIRE

Maps   OS Landranger 176 West London,186 Aldershot and Guildford.

From   Weybridge Station, Surrey.

To   Aldershot Station, Hampshire.

Distance 35km. Off-road 31km.

Route   After a short distance on the canalised river Wey this route branches west on the wholly artificial and newly restored Basingstoke Canal, cutting through sandy heathland to the garrison town of Aldershot in Hampshire. A gentle, level and entirely free of motor-traffic trip. Easy Navigation.

Railway Access
    BR Stations Weybridge, Woking, and Aldershot. Information 071 928 5100.

Places of Interest
    Brooklands Museum, Weybridge.

    Horsell Common, Woking.

    Aldershot - the military museums.

    The whole Basingstoke Canal.

Food and Drink
>Cafes, Weybridge.

>Carton's Cafe, Baker Street, Weybridge has tables outside (not Sunday).

>Kings Head PH, Guildford Road Bridge, Deepcut.

From Weybridge Station turn right for Brooklands Museum or left to descend Heath Road. Bear right into Church Street, on into the High Street (cafes and the Elmbridge Museum) then left at Monument Green into Thames Street to find the Old Crown PH at the corner of Thames Street and Walton Lane. Here a complex of basins, channels and islands marks the confluence of Thames and Wey.

From the north west you can get here via the Shepperton Ferry or from the north east via the Thames path. Turn down Church Walk footpath next to the Crown PH. Turn right into Jessamy Road, cross the old stream of the Wey on an iron bridge, over the access road on the island and continue down the narrow path opposite to emerge at Thames Lock where the Wey navigation begins. Cross the steep metal footbridge to reach the Wey towing-path.

Ham Haw Mill was built on this island in 1691 as a paper factory, it became an Iron works in 1720 and an oil-seed mill in 1842. It burned down in 1963 but the wooded site is still used for industry.

Follow the path on a causeway between the navigation and a run-off channel, across Colsons Bay weir. Pass under New bridge over a footbridge and up to cross Addlestone Road and continue past Town Lock. If you want to visit Weybridge turn left over the canal, the natural river and up Bridge Street. A left turn takes you into the town centre. Right at the end of Bridge Street for Weybridge BR and the Brooklands Museum.

Brooklands was originally conceived as a test-track when the motor-speed limit on public roads was 20mph. When persistent lobbying and law-breaking broke that prohibition it became the World's first banked motor-racing circuit - the Ascot of Motor-sport. It was also used for bicycle and motor-cycle racing and record breaking, and pioneer aviation. Many wonderful machines are housed in its restored buildings. The museums patron H.R.H. Prince Michael of Kent combines Presidency of the Institute of Road Safety Officers with convictions for motoring offences.

Pass Coxe's Lock and continue to the M25 Viaduct where a crossing of Woodham footbridge **(2km)** takes you onto the Basingstoke Canal.

The big building at Coxe's Lock is Coxe's Mill established in 1777 as an iron manufactuary, and subsequently a silk then corn-mill. The current structure, built in 1906 as a flour mill, was generating water-traffic until 1969 - corn coming up from London Docks. An attempted revival in 1981 was the last industrial haulage on this complex of waterways. Coxe's Mill was converted to housing in 1989. The mill pond behind it was aquired by the National Trust in 1993.

The Basingstoke Canal was built in 1794, much later than the Wey Navigation, and its character is entirely different. It does not follow a natural water-course but marches across country contemptous of the contours. It carried timber for ship and house building, grain, malt and other produce from North Hampshire and Surrey to London while coal and manufactured goods went the other way.

*At Monument Bridge **(13.5km)** you can cross the canal to visit Horsell Common, an extensive area of wooded country. There are prehistoric burial sites on either side of Monument Road and the common is only spoiled by noise from motor-traffic. On the other side of the canal is Woking whose town centre is rather uninspiring.*

The towing path follows the south bank of the canal then crosses to the north bank at Chobham Road. The path reverts to the south side at Kiln Bridge. Then goes back to the north side at Brookwood Bridge. At Pirbright Bridge **(21km)** it reverts to the south side.

From Pirbright Bridge the Canal rises 30 metres in only 2 miles. The 14 Locks of the Deepcut flight coming in quick succession. The area between two locks is called a pound and the Surrey summit pound of the Basingstoke Canal extends from the top of this flight all the way to Aldershot. It passes through a cutting over 20 metres deep shaded with mature Beech and Sweet chestnut trees. The high brick wall beyong the Curzon Bridge was built to sheild the hoses working the canal from passing trains which tended to frighten them.

The Basingstoke Canal was never a commercial success.

Water supplies to feed the Deepcut locks were often a problem and the absence of local industry meant that income was hardly sufficient to service the company's debts. In 1838 it enjoyed a boom during the construction of the London and South Western Railway from London to Portsmouth, when it was used to transport spoil and materials. Once the line was opened however it creamed off a good deal of freight. The tracks can be seen to the south and when the canal emerges it crosses over the railway on an aqueduct.

As it emerges beyond the highlands of the Surrey Heath the canal turns south to follow the valley of the Blackwater River, the Surrey/Hampshire border. At the Guildford Road (27km) bridge the path shifts to the western side of the cut.

The Guildford road bridge is built from Sarsen Stone excavated from the Deepcut. Beyond are only two more locks the level being maintained by an embankment, a further aqueduct and a tunnel. It was the decay of these works, the partial collapse of the Greywall Tunnel in 1932 left the Basingstoke canal four miles short of its name town, and the dramatic bursting of the Ash Embankment in 1968 led to the closure of the rest. Restoration began in 1973 and the waterway from the Wey to Greywall was reopen by 1988. It is unlikely to regain Basingstoke as the derelict tunnel is a now a protected bat roost (for more information 0252 370073). There is a small canal museum across the cut at Mytchett Place.

The bodies of water that appear on the east of the canal are Mytchett Lake and Great Bottom Flash. These natural heathland meres were enlarged to provide reservoirs for the canal. The last commercial traffic on the canal was timber to Woking in 1949.

At the Ash Vale Bridge **(31km)** - preceded by a pipe across the water-way - the canal intersects with the Hog's Back Ride to Guildford.

An army camp was first established at Aldershot in 1854 during the Crimean War. The surrounding area of Bagshot Heathland had little agricultural value and 10,000 acres were purchased for a permenant base. The canal was a significant factor in this choice since it provided a cheap way of transporting supplies from the armies other home at Woolwich. From 1854 and 1859 more than 20,000 tons of timber and slate were brought up the canal for the camps construction.

Leave the canal at the Government Road Bridge **(32.5km)** which comes after two rail bridges, at the end of the restored Ash Embankment. Cross the canal and follow and Government Road and Ordnance Road, turn right onto the High Street and left into Pickford Street then on up Arthur Rd to the Station **(35km)**.

Aldershot is the home of the British Army and contains The British Military Museum and several Regimental Museums.

88

10 THE GRAND JUNCTION
A long-haul via Southall

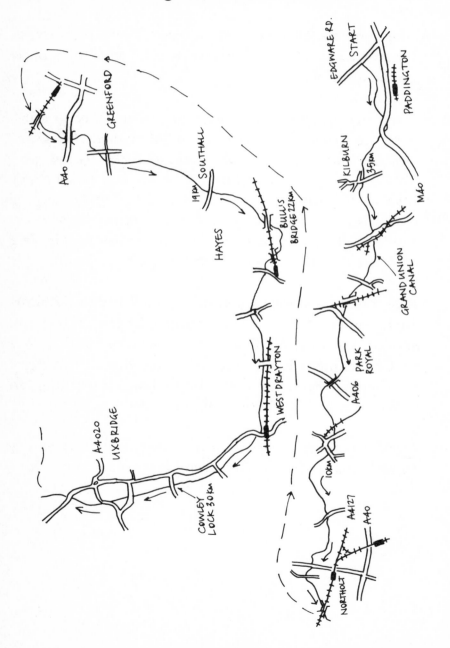

10 THE GRAND JUNCTION
A long-haul via Southall

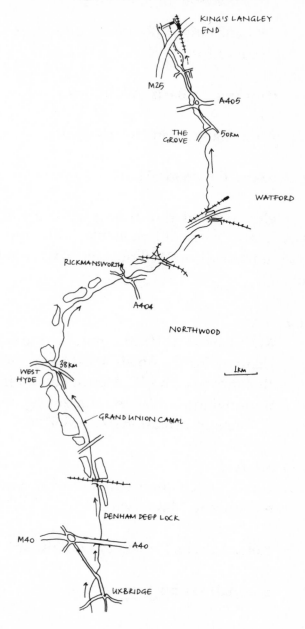

10 THE GRAND JUNCTION
A long-haul via Southall

Maps   OS Landranger 176 West London, 166 Luton and Hertford.

From   Paddington Basin, Westminster.

To   Kings Langley in Hertfordshire.

Distance 53km. Off-road 51km.

Route   Gentle canal side riding with few difficulties. A bell is useful to avoid possible collisions at blind corners, round bridges. Without one a warning shout is prudent.

Railway Access
     Marylebone or Paddington for the start. Kings Langley for the finish. West Drayton BR or Rickmansworth LRT Metropolitan Line provide optional interim abandonment points. BR Stations Information 071 928 5100.

Places of Interest
     Little Venice - houseboats and Regency elegance in Maida Vale.

     Kensal Green Cemetery - Gothic splendour.

     Southall - suburban exotica.

Colne Valley - green and isolated.

Cassiobury Park - Kingfishers in west Watford.

Food and Drink

Excellent Fish and Chips at the Sea Shell
Lounge in Lisson Grove close to Marylebone
Station - it has short opening hours (always the
sign of a good eatery).

Southall has a wide range of Indian Cuisine
with plenty of inexpensive takeaway shops.

The Fishery Inn by the canal at Harefield.

Kings Head PH, Hunton Bridge.

*The original terminus of the Grand Junction Canal was on the
Thames at Brentford but an arm to Paddington Basin at the
end of the New Road (New Road was built in 1756 to allow
cattle to reach Smithfield without going down Oxford Street
and now known as Euston Road) gave faster access to London
and, after the opening of the Regents Canal in 1820 the Docks
as well. The area around the Basin is known as Little Venice.*

Find the Regents Canal where it passes beneath the
Edgeware Road (Watling Street) in Maida Vale. Ride
down Bloomfield Road, left across the canal of
Westbourne Terrace Road, and right onto Delamere
Terrace. Join the towpath at the end of this road. Cycling
on the towpath is forbidden by the City of Westminster

who administer this section on behalf of the British Waterways Board, so legally you must walk until you reach the Ladbroke Grove - bridge 5 - (3.**5km)** from where more sensible regulations apply.

Beyond Ladbroke Grove Kensal Green Cemetery lies opposite the tow path on the North Bank. Get there by crossing bridge 5 and finding the gatehouse in the Harrow Road. It is a pleasant place to wander and distinguished by some exuberant monuments..The Heinz factory beyond Acton Lane has covered wharves which indicate it was once serviced with waterborne freight. Alas no longer.

Beyond the new aqueduct over the 'improved' North Circular and the River Brent, the canal goes under the Heathrow-bound Piccadilly Line. Beyond the newly reconstructed Manor Farm Road bridge **(10km)** the path becomes unpaved, though never too rough.

A canal here was proposed as early as 1580 to supply London with fresh water from the Colne at Uxbridge. That project was superseded by the New River and this section was begun during the 1790's and opened in 1801 as a corridor for freight, and some passenger traffic.

The canal turns south in a slow and faltering arc. Pass a distinctive modern concrete footbridge linking plying fields on both sides. At the next footbridge made of metal and fire damaged turn left **(19km)** if you wish to sample the delights of Southall - one of London's most distinctive suburbs. Turn right into Dane Road which brings you to the Broadway. Turn east (right) into the centre of London's largest and most concentrated Indian Community.

The colour and vitality of the Southall Broadway is exaggerated by its context, a rather grey pre-war suburb. Every shop has a display on the pavement. For the touring cyclist the restaurants and food shops are a priority. Stock up on brinjal bahji while pretending to be Josie Dew. The mysteries of distant continents - before you've even got to Heathrow.

When you are ready to continue. Go West down the Broadway and left by the Hanborough Tavern into Bankside to rejoin the Canal. A couple of kilometres takes you to the old Grand Junction Mainline at Bulls Bridge **(22km)**.

The canal has got here without the need for locks as it faithfully follows the 100ft contour. The policy of cutting to the contours meant slow travel but reduced the need for expensive engineering works in an era when canals' only competition were muddy roads where horsepower was 25 times less efficient.

A left turn leads via the River Brent to the Thames (interchange Breathing Spaces The Thames Towpath Ride). Turn right to continue to out of town. So far the bridges have been numbered upwards from Paddington now they are numbered from Braunston where the Grand Junction met the Oxford (they were subsumed into the Grand Union only in 1929). The next bridge is 200.

West Drayton Station passes on the far bank. This area was once a notable source of bricks which were floated into London to service the Nineteenth Century building boom. The old industry has been replaced by modern trading estates that utilise the canal as landscape feature rather than a piece of infrastructure.

At Cowley Lock **(30km)** the first since Paddington and the start of the long climb to the Chiltern summit the path crosses to the Western Bank.

The canal and the River Colne briefly share a channel near Uxbridge Lock where the architecture of 'The Quays' is '30's inspired post-modern. At the next Lock - Denham Deep - there is a cafe in the cottage. Above here the canal is isolated among woods and water. There are no motor-roads crossing for 3kms, just a tall railway viaduct with the tracks for High Wycombe. The flooded gravel pits dominate the valley around Harefield .

Beyond Harefield **(38.5km)** (interchange with Into the Chilterns Ride) the canal turns slowly eastwards passing into Hertfordshire above Stockers Lock. Rickmansworth lies across the valley.

Above Rickmansworth in the area of Batchworth Locks a dense network of waterways signals the confluence of the Chess, the Colne and the Gade. The canal turns north up the valley of the Gade. A tube train track further complicates matters. This is Betjeman's Metroland. Croxley Green stands to the north. Now a suburb of Watford the paper mill of the same name is gone and its boats no longer carry loads of paper to the City of London. Pass west Watford where the Kingfishers fly in

Cassiobury Park.

In Grove Park the path crosses to the east bank via steep bridge 163 **(50km)**. Beyond the motorway bridge is 162 (interchange with Into the Chilterns Ride). The canal is joined in the Gade Valley by the Euston Glasgow mainline all of which are dwarfed by the giant M25 viaduct built in 1984.

Here the canal company paid for passing through aristocratic estates by building ornate bridges like 164 whose graceful curves and castellated balustrades speak of an age when the possibility of harmony between art, science and commerce was last entertained.

If you leave the canal at bridge 162 and head east you will reach the Kings Head PH and the Kings Lodge restaurant. Go under bridge 159 and the new road bridge next to it. Turn left across the grass and left again in front of Trout Lake bungalow to cross the canal. Go through the Industrial Estate to reach a T junction where a right turn takes you to Kings Langley Station.

11 INTO THE CHILTERNS

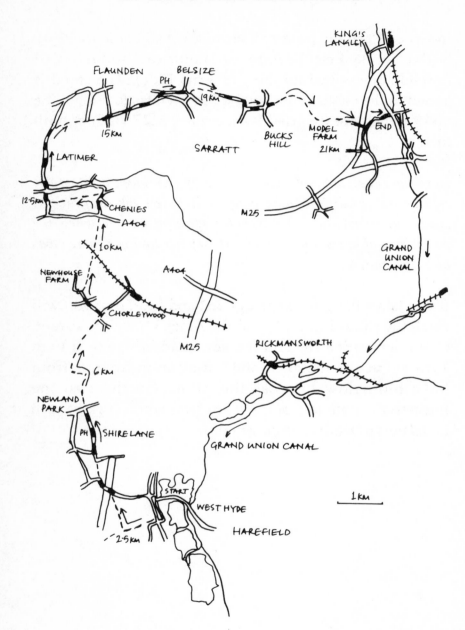

11 INTO THE CHILTERNS

Maps   OS Landranger 176 West London, 166 Luton and Hertford.

From   Grand Union Canal at Harefield.

To   Grand Union Canal at Hunton Bridge.

Distance 22.5km. Off-road 14km.

Route   This is a detour west from the Grand Union into the first of the Chiltern Hills. It provides extended sections of relatively remote off-road riding on well drained soils. Use the canal path to make a circular route.

Railway Access
      West Drayton for trains to Paddington. Kings Langley for Euston. Information 071 928 5100.

Places of Interest
      The Grand Union Canal.

      Chenies & Latimer - picturesque Buckinghamshire villages.

      Chess Valley - water meadows and bluebell woods.

      Chipperfield - village green and wooded common.

Food and Drink

Black Jack's Mill Restaurant, canalside at the start.

The Plough PH, Sarrat.

Two Brewers PH, Chipperfield.

The start is where Copper Mill Lane crosses the Grand Union Canal at West Hyde. From London ride the A404 Harrow Road/Rickmansworth Road then turn left onto White Hill just beyond the Mount Vernon Hospital. Follow signs for Harefield then go down Park Lane. Alternatively join the Canal at West Drayton (BR trains from Paddington) and ride north through Uxbridge. Leave the Canal at Black Jack's Mill Restaurant going west on Copper Mill Lane.

The Colne Valley has been excavated for gravel leaving its flat bottom as a string of lakes. The large derelict 19th century industrial complex on the East bank was a copper mill which manufactured sheeting to protect timber boats from worm attack.

Ride West down Coppermill lane between the lakes. At the Fisherman's Tackle pub turn left onto Old Uxbridge Road. Turn right onto the public footpath signposted for Shire Lane and cross the Main Road (Denham Way A412) with care. Follow the bridlepath ahead across farm land, to reach a cross after about one kilometre. Turn right **(2.5km)** up a steep hill on Shire Lane.

Harefield is the extremity of the old county of Middlesex. Buckinghamshire lies to the west and Hertfordshire to the north. In addition to the canal the Colne Valley carries three generatons of road. The Old Uxbridge Road, The Denham Way which 'relieved' it and the M25 which was meant to relieve that. Open for ten years the M25 is planned to be widened to become the largest highway outside North America - it looks increasingly unlikely that this plan will ever be executed or that it will ever be able to meet increasing traffic demands.

Shire Lane joins Chalfont Road. Turn Left to cross the M25. When Chalfont Road bends left carry straight ahead onto the narrow overgrown track. Emerge onto tarmac by a radio mast. Straight on past the Dumbbell PH. This is still Shire Lane. At the entrance to Newland Park College take the bridleway slightly to the right. Turn left at the T junction by the orange gate (6km), then right uphill with beech woods on your left.

The roller-coaster Shire Lane marks the county boundary. This route follows its line for 5km. On your right is Hertfordshire on your left Buckinghamshire.

As Shire Lane becomes 'macadamised once again we turn left into Buckinghamshire down Chalfont Lane. At the end of Chalfont Lane go straight on down the farm road towards Newhouse Farm. 30 metres before the famhouse fork right between wooden fences. Go straight on down into Carpenters Wood. Pass under the Metropolitan Line (10km). At the road (the A404 here called the Amersham Road) go straight across towards Chenies. Turn left on the bridleway by the primary school. Skirt the grounds of Chenies Manor before turning left to pass through a gate into the woods.

Set in splendid grounds Chenies Manor was enlarged in 1539 under the direction of John Russell the Lord High Admiral of England who served four Tudor monarchs and laid the foundation of the family fortune which persists to the present day. This is no longer their residence.

On re-joining the road turn right **(12.5km)** down steep Latimer Road and the over the river. Pass through Latimer then take the bridlepath which climbs steeply into the woods on the right. Go right as you enter the woods climbing a steep stony track. Follow the track round to the left and take another left at the crossroads in the hollow. Follow this to the small observatory. Go right on a rough often puddled farm lane which emerges onto tarmac as one arm of a staggered crossroads. Go forwards into Bragmans Lane. **(15km)**

Latimer lies in the valley of the Chess which strikes north-west into the Chilterns from the Colne at Rickmansworth. Famed for its watercress there are delightful riverside walks on either side of this route.

Descend Bragmans Lane and turn right onto Flaunden Lane at the little triangular green. Go straight ahead passed the Plough Inn then left up the lane marked with a cul-de-sac sign by the old-style red telephone box **(17km)**. When this lane forks go right onto Penmans

Green, a finger of common which becomes a narrow lane. At the Cart and Horses turn left onto Quickmoor Lane. At the T turn left onto Bucks Hill then right at the bridleway sign (**19km**).

Continue along Bucks Hill to find Chipperfield a mostly modern village with an extensive wooded common and the Two Brewers Pub reputed to have been a training centre for prize fighters in the 19th Century. There is cricket here on summer weekends.

At the end of the lush evergreen hedge go straight on. When you come to the footpath sign bear right down and along the dry valley bottom. When the track forks, swing left uphill to go ahead passed the mock-tudor Model Farm (**21km**). Turn left onto Langleybury Lane and descend to cross the A41 and rejoin the canal at bridge 162 (**22.5km**) just before the Kings Head PH (interchange with the Grand Junction Ride).

Turn right onto the towing path to complete a circular route back by rolling south to Harefield and the Thames. Turn left to go up to Kings Langley station (use directions in Grand Junction).

12 BY TWO WATERS TO TRING

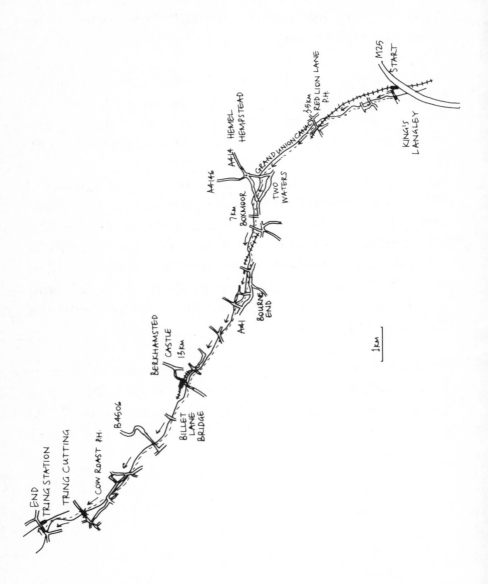

12 BY TWO WATERS TO TRING

Maps   OS Landranger 166 Luton and Hertford, 165
Aylesbury and Leighton Buzzard.

From   Kings Langley Station in Hertfordshire.

To   Tring Station in the Chiltern Hills.

Distance 19km. Off-road 18km.

Route   An ascent of the Chiltern Hills on the towing
path of the Grand Union Canal. Its whole length runs
parallel to the London to Birmingham mainline railway
making it a good ride for young children or anyone else
whose endurance may be unreliable. Easy navigation and
flat (locks and bridges excepted) with only slightly rough
going in places.

Railway Access
          Kings Langley, Hemel Hempstead,
          Berkhampstead and Tring, all served by trains
          from Euston. Information 071 928 5100.

Places of Interest
          Berkhampstead Castle - an impressive Norman
          ruin.

          Tring Museum - an over-stuffed annexe of the
          British Museum.

Tring Cutting - an early industrial earthwork.

Food and Drink
Fishery Inn, Boxmoor.

Castle Tea Room, High Street, Berkhampstead.

Cow Roast PH, Cow Roast.

Reach Kings Langley by train from Euston or via the canal (interchange with The Grand Junction Ride and Into the Chilterns Ride). Turn right out of the station and then first left down the new road into the industrial estate. Cross the canal bridge then turn right into the entrance to Trout Lake Bungalow with white gates and flag poles. Turn right again down the small grass valley between the bridge embankment and the white fence to join the towing path. Turn left (north).

The little river on the left is the Gade, which the canal follows through the ribbon-develpment of Nash Mills and Apsley. Food processing (limes were juiced at Two Waters), paper-mills and timber yards were all serviced by the canal. The canal, the railway and the old road to Banbury (until recently classified as the A41) share the valley. The road is now bypassed by a motorway running through the hills to the west. The water-meadows between the old factorys have been filled with new offices and 'out-of-town' stores. The first industrial complex on the right is still known the Ovaltine Factory although it was renamed Wander Foods in the 1970's.

Cross to the west bank of the canal at Red Lion Lane
(3.5km), where the pub of the same name is open all day,
and over to the east bank at bridge 154 - an elegant white
double arched structure - and back to the west at 153.

*Two Waters is the confluence of the Gade and the Bulbourne.
The canal follows the River Bulbourne west through Boxmoor.
Hemel Hempstead was, in living memory, a one-horse town
standing a mile up the Gade Valley from Two Waters. It was
identified as a site for a new town after the second world war
and expanded rapidly during the '50s and '60s to become a
settlement of more than 100,000 people sprawling across the
surrounding hills and absorbing several villages including
Boxmoor whose station was renamed. After passing under
bridge 150 the canal crosses what is left of the moor. On your
left is a pile of stones alledged to mark the grave of Robert
Snooks, highwayman, executed nearby.*

Turn left at the Fishery Inn **(7km)** at Boxmoor for Hemel
Hempstead Station.

*Beyond Old Fishery Lane, bridge 148, old water-cress beds line
the canal opposite the path. This was once a significant local
product. Winkwell has a busy drydock and low, timber hand-
operated swing bridge leading to the Three Horseshoes PH. A
few hundred metres of almost rural, almost quiet follows before
the canal enters Berkhampsted.*

Go under bridge 143 and then use it to cross to the north
bank. This pattern of progress allowed horses to cross
while harnessed to the boat. Pass the Boat and the Rising

Sun pubs and if you are travelling at night beware the steel barrier just before the Crystal Palace.

Leave the canal at bridge 141 **(13km)** and go through the railway embankment track to visit the castle or reach the station. The excellent Castle Tea Room is up Castle Street (not Mondays except Bank Holidays) in the other direction If you are carrying on cross to the south bank (here the canal is running westward) to go round the green.

Berkhampsted Castle was built by the Normans. Only scant flint ruins of the structure remain but the earthworks are spectacular enough not to be dwarfed by later feats of engineering - the canal cut or railway viaduct. The proximity of these three highlight the strategic value of this corridor through the Chilterns, whose steep gradients and dense woods were once a significant physical barrier. Across the river on Castle Street is Berkhampsted School, a minor public school where Graham Greene spent an awkward boyhood as the son of the Headmaster. The Totem Pole stands on the site of an old timber yard. It is modern, locally carved by a native Canadian.

Pass the Billet Lane bridge with its white painted direction to the Crooked Billet PH (interchange with Ashridge, Ivinghoe and the Tring Cutting Ride) There is no gap between Berkhampsted and the next village of Northchurch but beyond the canal finally breaks into open country. The Cow Roast Inn at bridge 137 **(17km)** offers camping facilities, its own marina and has given its name to the surrounding hamlet.

'Bournes' are rivers that only run in wet weather. Above the Cow Roast the Bulbourne no longer accompanies the canal. The Summit Pound that extends above Cow Roast Lock is filled with water pumped up from the extensive Tring Reservoirs over the hill. When the canal was busy water shortages were a constant problem. Boats would have to wait until a boat came in the other direction so that both could progress on the same lock full of water. Disputes with local millers were common.

The canal enters the quiet haven of Tring Cutting. Overgrown with mature trees, the green tranquility belies its man-made origins. Climb to bridge 135 **(19km)** (interchange with Ashridge, Ivinghoe and the Tring Cutting Ride) where a right turn takes you to Tring station. Tring, the last town in Hertfordshire is two miles in the other direction.

Tring Museum, the Natural-History Anexe of the British Museum is a red brick villa signposted from the centre of town. Every room is crowded with glass cases and every case stuffed with specimens from all over the world. Truly a gothic hallucination.

13 ASHRIDGE, IVINGHOE AND THE TRING CUTTING

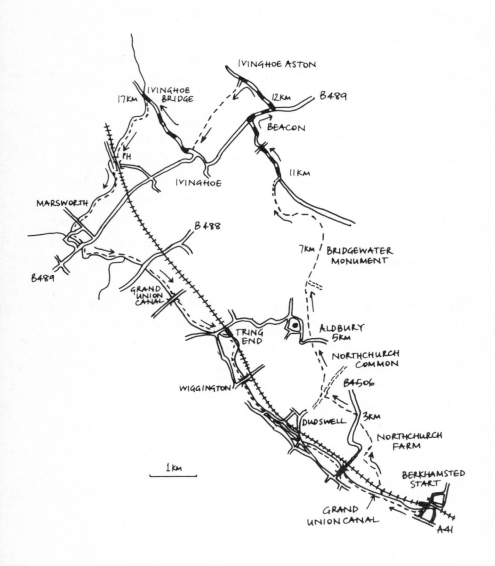

13 ASHRIDGE, IVINGHOE AND THE TRING CUTTING

Maps OS Landranger 165 Aylesbury and Leighton Buzzard.

From Berkhampsted Station in Hertfordshire.

To Tring Station via Ivinghoe Beacon.

Distance 25km. Off-road 5km.

Route Crossings of the Chiltern scarp on rough beech woodland tracks and back via the Marsworth Flight and Tring Cutting connected by a short ride on the Icknield Way. This route is hard. Lots of climbing and some rough - though mostly well drained - paths. The steep terrain demands careful navigation. A wrong turning resulting in unneccesary loss of height is no laughing matter.

Railway Access
BR Stations Berkhampstead and Tring.
Information 071 928 5100.

Places of Interest
Bridgewater Monument, Ashridge.

Ivinghoe Beacon - northern outpost of the Chilterns.

Pitstone Windmill and Farm Museum.

Ford End Watermill, Ivinghoe.

Tring Reservoirs The Marsworth Flight and the Tring Cutting.

Food and Drink
Castle Tea Rooms, Castle Street, Berkhampstead.

The White Lion PH, Marsworth.

From Berkhampsted Station (interchange Two Waters to Tring Ride) pass under the tracks and find the canal join the towing path at bridge 141 and turn right (north-west) At the modern Billet Lane bridge **(1km)** identified by the hand painted directions to the Crooked Billet PH leave the canal and turn right up the hill.

Cross the railway bridge and turn left onto Springfield Road. At the end of this road turn right then left into Crewe Curve and right onto a tarmac path between the houses. When the tarmac ends bear left into the Beech woods. Go ahead through the woods and on reaching a triangular junction go straight ahead. Continue straight ahead at Long Acre and straight ahead again at Northchurch Farm. Cross the road **(3km)** onto the bridleway which is quite indistinct among bracken. Carry on across Northchurch Common with open ground on your right. At the corner of the open ground enter the trees taking the path heading slightly to the right. Turn right before the big brick building of Norcott Hall Farm. At the white gates take the path to your right into the woods.

This is the fringe of the Ashridge Estate a large area of woodland administered by the National Trust.

Follow this path, which is either wet and soft or bumpy with dried hoof prints. Cross the road **(5km)** and continue into the woods on the other side. Cross the drive to a little woodland cottage and continue until the land begins to fall away giving views along the Chiltern Scarp.

From here until the route reaches Ivinghoe it follows permissive bridleways not public rights of way. Respect the rights of pedestrians to enjoy them quietly.

Turn up to the right and after about 20 metres find a good quality double-track path. Turn left and continue along the edge of the woods amid mature beeches. The path climbs up and emerges onto a lawn before the arresting sight of the Bridgewater Monument **(7km)**.

During the afternoons from April to October, for a fee, you can climb this doric collumn topped with an urn for a fine vista across the brickfields of Buckinghamshire. The tower was erected in 1832 in homage to Francis, Third Duke of Bridgewater. His costly speculation, seventy years before, in digging a cut from the Worsley coal mines to the centre of Manchester was much ridiculed as a costly folly - until it finally opened and began to produce such awesome profits that England was soon engulfed in canal-mania.

Cross the lawn to the foot of the tower and continue on into the woods. Fork right beyond the wooden gate **(9km)** and on reaching the grass car-park turn left and follow its upper edge. At the other end go through the timber bollards and follow the chalk track winding down to join the road. From here you can walk out to the Beacon summit.

It is not the height of Ivinghoe Beacon that made it a signal hill but its isolation as an outpost of the Chiltern Scarp. Ivinghoe Beacon is the starting point of the Ridgeway a long distance path that runs down to Avebury. North-east of the Thames much of the route is on footpaths but by following the Icknield Way at the foot of the scarp it is possible to ride on lanes or green roads from here all the way to Wiltshire. To the right you can see into Bedfordshire and the White Lion of Whipsnade, a modern chalk figure on Dunstable Downs.

Turn left on the road **(11km)**. Descend to the T junction and turn right on the busy B489. Turn left at the first junction **(12km)**. At the threshold of Ivinghoe Aston turn left onto a bridleway, fork right onto the unmetalled Lower Icknield Way.

The old market village of Ivinghoe and the neighbouring settlement of Pitstone, which grew to house the workers at the big cement factory, contain a reconstructed timber windmill dating from 1624, a farm museum and the Ford End watermill which ground flour till 1970.

On entering Ivinghoe turn right then right again **(15km)**

to run out passed the watermill to join the canal at Ivinghoe Bridge **(17km)**. Turn left on the towing path.

The canal here is 100 metres above sea level and has to climb twenty more metres to reach the summit pound in a couple of twisting miles. The main climb is made via the Marsworth Flight - seven consecutive locks. The reservoir dug to feed these locks and those descending on the south eastern side is now a haven for wildlife, particularly water birds. There is a 3km nature trail around the reservoir.

Follow the canal through Marsworth and climb the locks toward the summit. There is a path on both sides of the cut above bridge 131 **(21km)** and the White Lion PH. The path on the right is smoother but make sure you keep on the mainline as the Aylesbury Arm and then the Wendover Arm branch off to the west.

The Aylesbury Arm of 1814 is the start of the unfinished Western Junction Canal which was intended to reach the Thames at Abingdon. Above it the Wendover Arm had a different primary purpose; to collect water from Chiltern streams to feed the canal. The canal network introduced national communication on a scale not seen since the Roman era. The brickbuilt workshops at the summit show the scale of the operation.

Continue through Tring Cutting, leave the tow path at bridge 135 for Tring Station **(25km)** or Town, (interchange Two Waters to Tring Ride) or continue down the canal to Berkhampsted.

Tring cutting was dug with picks and shovels. The spoil was hauled in barrows up wooden plank 'horse-runs'. The horse stood on top of the cutting and pulled the barrow via a pulley. The barrow was steered by a navigator (Navigator was the contemporary euphemism for a canal labourer, origin of the diminutive navvy.) who was attached to the barrow by a harness.

14 OVER BARNET TO ST ALBANS

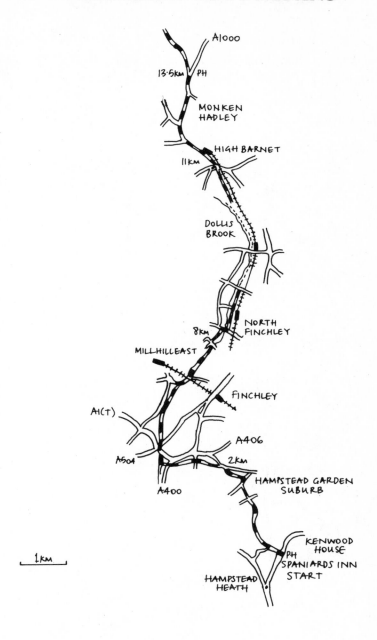

14 OVER BARNET TO ST ALBANS

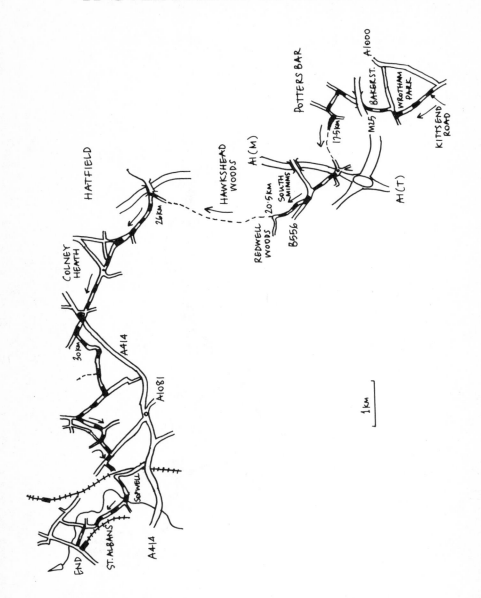

14 OVER BARNET TO ST ALBANS

Maps   OS Landranger 176 West London, 166 Luton and Hertford.

From   Hampstead Heath.

To   St Albans in Hertfordshire.

Distance 37km. Off-road 16km.

Route   The southern section of this diverting exit from north London follows the upper River Brent to Barnet. There is a stretch of lovely woodland riding beyond South Mimms but the real point is to get to St. Albans, a tourist destination to match any in Nothern Europe. This ride involves negotiating some busy roads particularly through Barnet and London Colney. Its only dirty section is Bridgefoot lane.

Railway Access
St. Albans for trains to Luton and St Pancras.

Hampstead Heath, on the North London Line. Information 071 928 5100.

Places of Interest
Hampstead Heath - north London's green lung.

Kenwood House - a public art gallery on Hampstead Heath.

High Barnet - an ancient hilltop town on the
Great North Road.

St. Albans - birthplace of the Campaign for Real
Ale.

Food and Drink
Cafe in the converted stables at Kenwood
House.

Lots of choice in Barnet High Street.

Even more in St Albans.

*Hampstead Heath (interchange Breathing Spaces London's
Parks & Regent's Canal Ride) is an area of high ground whose
springs provide the source of the River Fleet. It is large enough
(800 acres) and wild enough to give a real sense of open country
with fresh water ponds for swimming (M, F and mixed). It is
traversed by a network of paths but only a couple of them are
open to cycle-traffic.*

Get to the top of Hampstead Heath **(1km)** on the bike path
which begins opposite the end of Downshire Hill. Use
Millfield Lane which runs up from Highgate Ponds or
take the Parkland Walk from Finsbury Park. Climb
Jacksons Lane into Highgate then out along Hampstead
Lane. Walk down through the steep woods on the north
side of Spaniards Lane between the Spaniards Inn and
Manor House Hospital. Turn right on reaching Wildwood
Road and follow it down beside the playing fields that

form the northernmost outpost of Hampstead Heath into Hampstead Garden Suburb.

Hampstead Garden Suburb, an early 20th Century experiment in town planning was built on land purchased by local philanthropist and yimby (yes in my back yard) Dame Henrietta Barnet. Here people of all classes were meant to live harmoniously side by side. The street plan is laid out to respect the contours and its tree lined avenues and closes were used as a model for New Towns built later in the Century. There are no pubs.

Wildwood Road progresses into Thornhill Way. Turn right into Northway and left into Oakwood Crescent. Find Mutton Brook between Addison Way and the North Circular **(2km)**. Follow the 'green chain' riverside path Westward until Mutton Brook joins Dollis Brook **(3.5km)** where it turns north.

These muddy and narrow riverside paths are primarily for pedestrians; use them to avoid the maze of big motor-roads which dissect the area but go carefully and be prepared to walk. When the path crosses Hendon Lane you can use the parallel suburban roads listed below, or keep to the scenic riverside on foot.

Turn right onto Hendon Lane, left onto Broughton Avenue, left onto Waverly Grove. Right onto Holders Hill Drive. Right onto Holders Hill (B552), right into Thornfield Avenue, left into Dollis Road - under the Northern Line Viaduct - left into Gordon Road, straight on into Brent Way, Field Road, Westbury Road and Holden Road. Then turn left down Laurel View and right **(8km)** onto the Dollis Brook path across Whetstone Stray.

Dollis Brook is the infant River Brent. This section forms the boundary between the ancient parishes of Hendon to the west and Finchley to the east. (For more information on the Dollis Brook Path ring Barnet Council on 081 446 8511 ext 4478). If you are in a hurry to shrug off suburbia the former Great North Road (the A1000) runs north from Highgate to Barnet on high ground to the east.

Beyond Upper Whetstone Stray and Brook Farm Open Space turn right then left onto Grasvenor Avenue. Continue into Fairfield Way then left to join the Great North Road **(11km)** at Barnet Hill which climbs to Barnet.

Chipping or High Barnet was once a Hertfordshire Market Town and now gives its name to a London Borough. It is the highest hill on the Great North Road between London and York. Plenty of old inns testify to its history as the first town on the road North. It is halfway between London and St. Albans. It has an Art Centre a range of cafes and restaurants. You can picnic on Hadley Green at the Northern end of the High Street. Beyond the Green stands a stone obelisk which commemorates a fight on the 14th of April 1471 in which Edward IV's gang defeated the Earl of Warwick's. Warwick was killed in the process.

Go north through Barnet ignoring the left forks of Wood Street and the St. Albans Road. Fork left at the 'Battle of

Barnet monument stone **(13.5km)** onto Kitts End Road. At the T turn right onto Dancers Hill and left on to Baker Street. Under the M25 take the second left, Santers Lane, round a giant one-way system designed to inconvenience cyclists, to find the bridleway Bridgefoot Lane **(17.5km)**. This muddy track leads to a brick bridge over Mimshall Brook. On regaining tarmac turn left on Swanland Road, right over the A1M then left up Greyhound Lane to South Mimms.

Caught in a tourniquet of motorways South Mimms could be the noisiest village in England.

Go straight ahead through the village onto Blackhorse Lane to lose the growl of motor-traffic among its trees. At the top of this road **(20.5km)** carry straight on through the brick pillars into Redwell Wood. Watch out for galloping horses. Follow the firm but bumpy track to North Mimms Church. Turn left onto Tollgate Road and **(26km)** go straight through Colney Heath. Further progress demands crossing the dual carriageway A405 although the ramped footbridge is an alternative for the timid to regain the line of Colney Heath Lane.

The source of the river Colne is close to North Mymms. The Lee runs just north of Hatfield about 5 miles to the north east. Geologists think that the Thames once ran this way in a great loop north of the London Basin using the valleys of the Colne and the Lee. It was - so the theory goes - only during the last ice-age when this course was obstructed by an ice sheet that the new 'direct' line between Staines and Barking appeared.

Turn left **(30km)** onto Barley Mow Lane. Turn right onto Highfield Lane, left onto Hill End Lane, left onto Drakes Drive then right onto Admiral's Walk a service road to Watling Street which here runs as the main London to St. Albans motor road. Cross at the traffic lights into Cotton Mill Lane to descend past the mill at Sopwell **(34km)**.

The abandoned pub in Barley Mow Lane fails to confirm the shaky theory that new roads bring prosperity. Be warned the prospect of St. Albans Abbey from Cottonmill Lane could turn you Christian.

As Cottonmill Lane (interchange with Hertford St Albans Ride) recrosses the River Ver on the outskirts of St. Albans turn left on the riverside path by the old Municipal Baths. At the next road turn right then left by the Duke of Marlborough PH then left just bellow the Junior School onto a dirt track that leads to the Abbey Orchard and the Old Fighting Cocks PH **(37km)**.

St. Albans is a brilliant destination, with attractions too numerous to list here - but you'd have to be pretty unimaginative not to enjoy the Roman amphitheatre. Interesting museums are plentiful not to mention various bun shops. It has several pubs worthy of the birthplace of the Campaign for Real Ale. Trains carry bikes to St. Pancras except in the morning rush hour. Tourist information St. Albans 64511.

15 THE LOST LINK

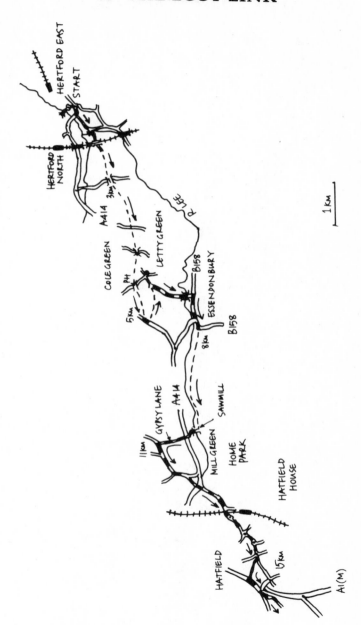

15 THE LOST LINK

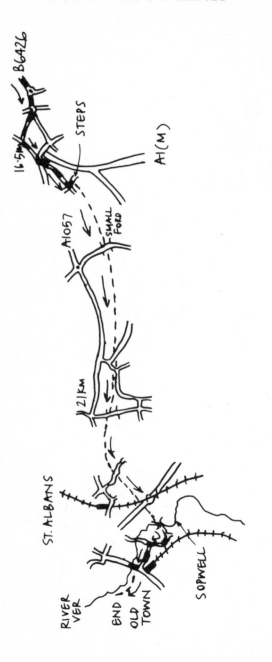

15 THE LOST LINK
Hertford to St Albans

Maps   OS Landranger 166 Luton and Hertford.

From   Hertford North or East Stations.

To   St Albans.

Distance 25km. Off-road 18km.

Route   This level ride begins with a section of overgrown railway on the banks of the Lee. A somewhat surreal traverse of Hatfield brings it to another abandoned line which leads through ribbon development to the heart of Old St Albans. The ride is easily ridden in all weathers, apart from the short section West of Essendonbury which can be soft but is never seriously muddy. Crossing Hatfield New Towns involves negotiating a series of traffic-islands.

Railway Access

BR Station Hertord North for trains to Finsbury Park and Kings Cross. Hertford East to Liverpool Street via Broxbourne. St. Albans for St. Pancras. Information 071 928 5100.

Places of Interest

Hertford - where Alfred the Saxon defeated the Danes.

The Lee bank between Essendonbury and Mill Green.

Mill Green Museum - a restored corn mill.

Hatfield House - massive Tudor Palace and grounds.

St Albans - the most interesting town in south east England.

Food and Drink

Pubs and Cafes, Hertford.

The Cowper Arms, Cole Green is open all day.

Cafeteria in Verulamium - the riverside park in St Albans.

Hertford stands at the head of the River Lee Navigation but the Lee itself continues to its source near Luton. It is joined here by the Mimram the Beane and the Rib rivers. Water as a means of communication and source of power was instrumental in Hertford's development. It claims Britain's first paper mill dating from 1488. The Castle (a municipal building on the site of Norman fortifications) contains a tourist information office and the formal grounds are a quiet picnic spot.

From the centre of Hertford find West Street whose only access is from the westbound carriageway of Gascoigne Way. Go to the roundabout at the south end of The Wash and turn right. If you don't fancy riding on an urban expressway for 300 metres take the subway from Castle Street towards the Courthouse then walk right along the footway.

West Street is rather forlorn now that its function as an approach to the town is degraded. It has some fine 17th and 18th Century houses but hangs off Gascoigne Way like a withered limb.

West Street becomes Horn Lane (interchange with Wildwoods Above the Lee Ride). As this bends left, take the track down to the right. Follow the Lee Valley Walk signs and cross the river on a timber bridge. Go straight ahead by the horse jumping field. This leads under the viaduct carrying the trains to Hertford North station and into woods. Join the Cole Green Way and turn left.

The old railway to Welwyn Junction follows the Lee valley and has been converted into a walking and cycling route named after its present terminus Cole Green.

When the track bed runs into a short cutting (3km) the overhead bridge has gone so you must climb up and down (the steps going down the otherside are steep and deep) to continue. Keep straight on at the car-park at the old Cole Green Station site unless you want to deviate to the Cowper Arms a few metres to the North. The Cole Green Way terminates at the A414 'improved' motor road. Turn left and left again after a few metres (5km) onto the green lane. On reaching the road at Letty Green turn right and continue on tarmac over the River Lee. Turn right onto the B158 at the T junction. At Essendonbury the road turns left out of the valley go ahead onto the drive to the pumping station and pick up the bridleway going into the trees on the left (**8km**). Follow the bridleway through farmland along the Lee's Southern bank.

Above Hertford the Lee's character changes. It does not support an artificial cut, complex of drainage channnels and reservoirs and is now a single wandering lowland river. The path brings you to the limits of the grounds of Hatfield House. The saw mill processes one of the estates crops. Corn has been ground at Mill Green for a thousand years. The restored watermill is now a public museum.

Continue ahead parallel to the river when the path meets a perfect blacktop drive. Cross the River by the sawmill then cross the A414 Hertford Road into Gypsy Lane. At the T Junction turn left into Ascots Lane (**11km**). Turn left onto the cycle-track running beside the A1000. Follow this track across to the other side of the road and on into Hatfield. Go straight ahead at the lights into St. Albans Road East (Interchange with Breathing Spaces The Lea and The Mimram Ride). A left turn takes you to the entrance of Hatfield House.

The old road to York and Edinburgh crosses the Lee in this area and its shifting lines over the years have had some bizarre consequences. At the traffic lights on the approach to Hatfield New Town the cul-de-sac on the right is The Great North Road which crosses the railway on a footbridge. Shame that as the old coach roads have been bypassed and re-bypassed their direct lines have not been maintained for cycle-traffic. Traffic roundabouts are the distinctive feature of the post-war New Towns and Hatfield is no exception. The swimming pool by the junction of Cavendish Way has a hyperbolic-paraboloid roof.

At the roundabout follow the signs for St Albans (B6246) onto Queensway the second exit. At the next roundabout take the third exit, still Queensway. At the next roundabout go straight ahead onto Cavendish Way then turn right **(15km)** onto St Albans Road West.

The former A1 is now bypassed by a cut-and-cover tunnel running beneath Le Galleria, a mall which despite its pretentious European title is an example of Californification (stark low density development to accommodate the motor car). The Hatfield Tunnel was based on plans for the M11 Link in East London which was started in 1993 after forty years of planning but not as a tunnel which was considered too expensive. The Comet roundabout is named after the Hotel which is named after Hatfield's most famous product, the World's first jet airliner. The former de Havilland works and airfield stand to the west.

Pick your way through Galleria's sterile environs and turn South (left) on the A1001. At the Comet Roundabout go ahead following signs for Colney Heath. After about 200 metres stop cross and take the steps down on the right **(16.5km)** to join Selwyn Crescent. Taking a line from the bridge go ahead through the modern housing estate to find a stymie gate next to the Ellenbrook Recreation area.

This is the entry to a second stretch of track-bed which runs all the way to St Albans.

This railway conversion which dates from 1985 is named the Smallford Trail after a hamlet midway between St. Albans and Hatfield. Running level through ribbon development it is made pleasant and scenic by a green tunnel of overhanging trees. The small ford in question was over a tributary of the Colne so we have made it from one river system to another on the reputed former course of the Thames.

After two bridges overhead and a level crossing emerge by an old factory. Cross Sutton Road **(21km)** and climb steps to re-enter trees and pass a stupendously derelict factory on the right. After the cemetery exit left then turn right into Dellfield and go up the tarmac path on the right to rejoin the track-bed. Go under the mighty brick arch of the tracks to St Pancras and under Watling Street (the A1081) loop around to the left ignore the steps and stay on the path onto a single-track section. Go under a bridge then turn left back up to the track. Cross the river Ver then after going under a last brick bridge go round to the right past Sopwell Youth Club to emerge onto the road. Turn right onto Cotton Mill Lane **(23km)** and make an entry into the heart of the old city using the last section of the Barnet to St Albans Route to finish at the Fighting Cocks PH **(25km)**.

16 WILDWOODS ABOVE THE LEE

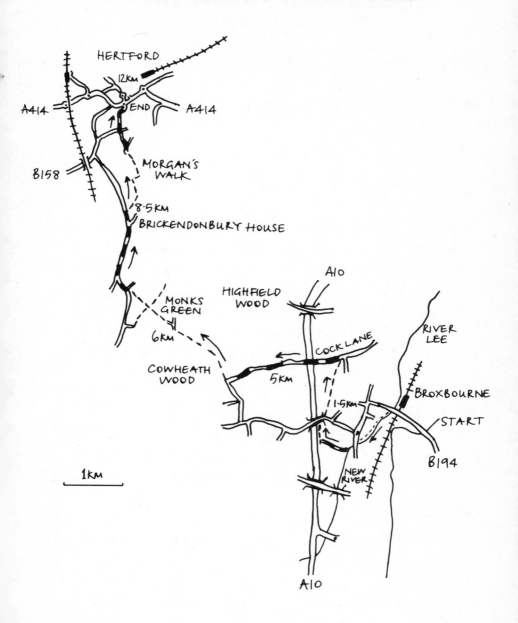

16 WILDWOODS ABOVE THE LEE
Broxbourne to Hertford

Maps   OS Landranger 166 Luton and Hertford.

From   The River Lee at Broxbourne.

To   Hertford.

Distance 12km. Off-road 7km.

Route   Climbing away from the Lee and the New
River the route crosses woodland on good forest paths.
The second section is on dirty bridleways across farmland
followed by a descent to rejoin the river at Hertford. The
off-road sections are tough but mostly rideable
interspersed with respite sections on tarmac lanes. This
route can be extended to form a circular tour using the
towing path of the river Lee.

Railway Access
        BR Stations Broxbourne and Hertford North
        and East, for trains to Liverpool Street or
        Finsbury Park. Information 071 928 5100.

Places of Interest
        Broxbourne Church - on the banks of the New
        River.

        Martin's Green - a wooded hamlet.

Brambles Woods - wild and lonely.

Hertford - historic County town with a
gruesome bypass.

Food and Drink

Not much on offer on this lonely ride.

A selection of Cafes and Pubs in Hertford.

The Newsagent in The Wash (opposite the
Castle) sells snacks and sandwiches and is open
on Sundays.

Get to the start of this ride by extending the River Lee
section of the Kings Cross to Watham Cross Ride.
Cheshunt is south of the start, Broxbourne BR Station is
also nearby. If you are coming north on the tow path turn
left on a narrow channel opposite Broxbourne rowing
club. If you are coming from the station turn right onto
Station Road then left towards the Church to join Mill
Lane.

*The Old Mill buildings at the foot of Mill Lane are gone but
some of the works, including a big water driven wheel can still
be seen, protected by a brick structure. St Augustines Church
standing beside the New River is the last resting place of John
Mcadam the great improver of British roads who lived out his
last years (1823-1836) in nearby Hoddesdon. His
'Macadamising' process, the fore-runner of tarmacadam allowed
road transport to flourish briefly , before the 19th Century*

railway boom.

Climb Mill Lane and turn left (walking) onto the footpath running beside the New River. Negotiate the awkward gate and turn left onto High Road the old Hertford (and Cambridge) road. Turn right into Cozen's lane West, cross the New River and continue up onto Wormley Playing Fields then turn right on the trotting-track above the new A10 (Hoddesdon By-Pass). On rejoining tarmac turn briefly right down Bell Lane then left **(1.5km)** at the big old oak into Allard Way which becomes a bridleway running behind the houses of upper Broxbourne. Turn left into Cock lane.

South east Hertfordshire still retains a good deal of the dense decidous forest that once covered most of South East England. The trees along Cock Lane are mostly Hornbeam which have in the past been coppiced to provide timber for fencing or firewood.

Just beyond Martin's Green (intersection with the New River & Ermine Street Ride) where the road bends left **(5km)** at a row of cottages turn right to pass the green painted metal water-tower on a forest path. After a lonely descent and climb through Bramble's Wood fork right in a clearing through a galvanised gate and turn left on the road. Pass carefully through Monk's Green Farmyard **(6km)** and after the buildings fork right down a muddy single-track bridleway marked with a red arrow, between dense hedges.

Miniature ponies are usually grazing in the Monk's Green farm's home field. Popular with children and sentimental photographers. The path beyond Monk's Green is always wet. In Winter it runs as a stream but since it inclines down and the surface is firm it can almost always be negotiated awheel. The right turn off this bridleway, signposted for Mangrove Road, may be the toughest 800 metres of public right of way in South East England. Don't try it alone after wet weather. It holds puddles in which you could loose your bike or your life.

Turn right when you reach tarmac, onto Brickendon Lane. Just after the entrance to Brickendon Bury a grand house now used as a laboratory turn right **(8.5km)** on a bridleway across a concrete bridge. The path rises crossing an open field diagonally. Go through the gate with a style on its left and follow the next field's edge keeping the hedge on your right. At the corner of the next field go straight on to the lone finger-post in the centre. Turn right to reach the belt of trees on the right known as Morgan's Walk. On reaching this dilapidated tree-lined avenue turn left for Hertford.

On reaching the urban fringe go straight on into Morgan's Road, turn left into Peggs Lane to emerge opposite County Hall **(10km)**. Turn right to descend into Hertford. At the bottom of the hill turn right into Horn Lane which becomes West Street and leads back into the town.

Hertford had the misfortune to be redeveloped at the height of the car age and it is now filleted for the benefit of motor traffic. Gascoigne Way a nondescript dual-carriageway bars entry. The

136

hardy can shoulder their bikes, dodge the speeding motor-traffic and climb two barriers (this is what is called 'progress').

Otherwise you turn left to ride to the next roundabout before being able to penetrate the town centre by turning right and right again. The third alternative is to take the footpath to the right and use the subway by the Law Courts to get into Castle Street **(12km).**

The irony is that rush hour congestion now has the County Council pressing for a new bypass for the existing bypass through the fields our route has just crossed (more information from Hertford Against Road Madness - HARM 0992 586 252). Hertford - once you can get into it - is a pleasant little town. The downtown area is a muddle of one-way operation and bike bans which are being modified at the time of writing. Hertford East station is found at the end of Railway Street where there is a seven-day Halfords. Hertford North is at the other end of town on the road to Stevenage.

Pass the East station to get to Dickersons Mill where a right turn on the River Lee towing Path takes you back to Kings Meads, Ware, Broxbourne or even London.

17 NEW RIVER & ERMINE STREET

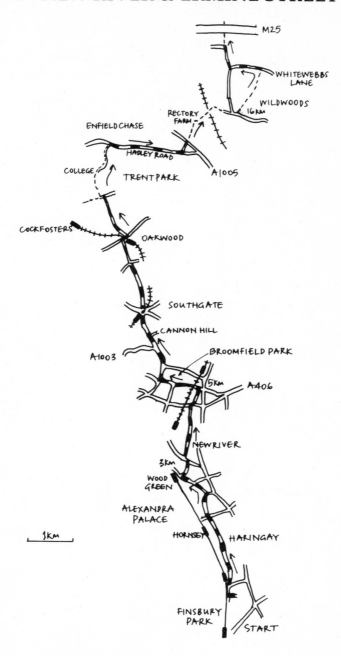

17 NEW RIVER & ERMINE STREET

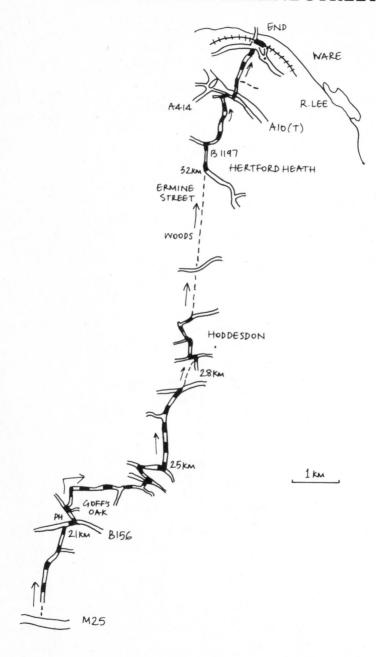

17 NEW RIVER & ERMINE STREET

Maps   OS Landranger 176 West London, 166 Luton and Hertford.

From   Finsbury Park.

To   Ware, Hertfordshire.

Distance 35km. Off-road 12km.

Route   An undulating tour from the fringe of Inner London into the wooded highlands of Hertfordshire. The first urban miles follow the New River (which is neither new nor a river). Further north we use the long abandoned line of Ermine Street - the Roman's Road to York. The ride is rarely flat and the heavy clay is hard work; expect to walk for extended sections in winter.

Railway Access

     BR Stations Finsbury Park, Ware. Information 071 928 5100.

Places of Interest

     Finsbury Park - one of London's oldest public parks.

     Alexandra Palace - a 19th Century temple to commerce.

     Temple Bar - in Theobalds Park, a transplanted City landmark.

Ermine Street.

Ware - Hertfordshire malting town.

Food and Drink

Seven day shopping for Cypriot fruit and cake in Green Lanes.

Nobbie's Cafe in Ware High street is open seven days a week.

Finsbury Park was one of the first areas of open country reserved for the recreation of London's commoners It was bought by the Borough of Finsbury (which lies just North of the City of London and is now part of Islington) as that area's fields and gardens disappeared under buildings during the nineteenth century. It contains a hilly road circuit once used for top class cycle-racing, suitable for fitness training on a bike. A useful route centre for cyclists, it is connected with central London by the Kings Cross to Waltham Cross Ride and the starting point of the Parkland Walk (interchange with Breathing Spaces London's Parks & Regent's Canal Ride). The New River whose construction was a key influence on the growth of London runs through the Park.

Leave Finsbury park by the Hornsey Gate at its North Western corner. Turn right into Endymion Road and left into Alroy Road which becomes Wightman Road. Cross Turnpike Lane into Hornsey Park Road and left into Mayes Road and left again into Station road with a view across Wood Green Common to Alexandra Palace

Alexandra Palace was built in 1873, the previous building completed in 1862 burned down sixteen days after opening. In the years since it has been used as an Exhibition venue, barracks, prisoner of war camp, TV transmitter and studio. Today it still hosts exhibitions, including "Bicycle Expo" in October, dry skiing and ice-skating.

Station Road crosses the New River as it enters a tunnel. Turn right onto Park Avenue, then left onto the open ground on the left following the line of the underground waterway. Follow the strip of grass across Bounds Green Road **(3km)** until it reaches Nightingale Road. Turn right and left onto Finsbury Road which becomes Palmerston Road. Cross Myddleton Road. The New River has emerged from the tunnel and runs behind the houses on the left.

The New River was dug 10ft wide and 4ft deep in the early 17th Century to bring fresh water from springs near Hertford to the cholera ridden dwellings of London. Its construction, under the direction of the wealthy goldsmith Hugh Myddelton, allowed London's suburbs to expand northwards. The serpentine 'river' followed the 100ft contour for 39 miles although a straight line from head to tail measured little more than twenty. Some of the loops were removed in the 19th Century The tunnel followed here was built in 1852 and cut out a long loop to the east through Edmonton. The section south of Finsbury Park was closed in 1946.

Cross the North Circular into Palmerston Crescent then left as this meets Green Lanes **(5km)**. (Riders keen to get quickly into the country can come direct from Finsbury Park on Green Lanes, the longest street in London - not at all green and notorious for bad driving.) Turn first left past Palmers Green Library into Broomfield Lane. Follow the Lane round Broomfield Park into Powys Lane and up Cannon Hill through Southgate.

At Southgate Circus go straight on down Chase Road and up to Oakwood Station where the chip shop and bakers offer a last chance to buy food before the serious off-road begins. Turn right into Bramley Road and left down Snakes Lane into Trent Park.

Trent Park, was once part of Enfield Chase Royal Hunting Forest. It is now a country park containing a campus of Middlesex University, formerly Middlesex Polytechnic.

When you reach the campus go straight on until you find the stop sign, then turn left past the obelisk with the pineapple on the top. Just before the 12mph speed limit sign turn right (**11km**) down the loose stone path. This surface requires extreme care - no sudden steering or braking - walking is allowed and cycling may not be - so don't speed. At the bottom of the hill bear right round the ornamental lake then follow the signs for Hadley Road. The path is steep but the surface is good enough to be ridden if you have the determination.

The water pumping station in Hadley Road is another Nineteenth Century addition to London's water supply. Water was drawn from underground porous rocks to feed the New River which by then had been widened. Another pumping station in Whitewebbs Lane is being converted into a transport museum.

Turn right down Hadley Road and pass the water pumping station. Turn left into Oak Avenue, right onto the Ridgeway and left onto the bridleway to Rectory Farm. Take care through the farmyard then continue up under the railway line from Finsbury Park to Hertford. Where the path divides turn right into Strayfield Lane. This track meets Theobalds Park Road between the Fallow Buck Pub and St John's Church. Cross the road **(16km)** into Flash Lane rattle down to Cuffley Brook and up through the woods to Whitewebbs Lane.

The New River used to flow in a Westward loop through the woods at the bottom of Flash Lane. In wet weather its original course holds water and the remains of it can be seen on the North side of the natural stream Maidens Brook. The tip of the loop was cut off by a cast-iron and brick aqueduct running parallel to Flash Lane in 1820. A much bigger aqueduct made the whole loop redundant in 1859. Theobalds Park, reached by a right turn on White Webbs Lane and a left into Bulls Cross Ride, was the site of a house belonging to James I. Theobalds Road WC1 was part of the King's route from Westminster to this significant country seat. A gateway (and toll booth) to the City of London designed by Christopher Wren, which marked Temple Bar at the western end of Fleet Street, now stands's isolated in woods on the line of Ermine Street in Theobalds Park. It was moved in 1888 when the High Court was built in the Strand, to allow vehicle traffic unrestricted access to the City. Following the success of modern traffic restraint in the

*City of London - 'the ring of lego' - it may be time to return it
to London. Theobalds Park also contains a fine curving section
of the New River and Capel Manor Environmental Centre
(0992 763849) with an open farm, woodland walks and a
campsite.*

Unless you are going to visit Theobalds Park turn left
down White Webbs Lane, right onto Theobalds Park road
and, when it bears left, straight on onto the bridle path
signposted 'Glasgow Stud'. Follow this line for three
kilometers of rough lane passing under the M25 to emerge
onto **(21km)** Jones Road at Goff's Oak.

*The straight lanes and isolated brick built farms of this area
(still part of the Theobalds Park Estate) show that this land was
enclosed for agriculture fairly late. The housing estates and
glass houses of Goff's Oak are scattered on hills between Cuffley
and Cheshunt and no obvious route through them makes for
2km of tricky north-south navigation.*

Turn right onto Cuffley Hill and left into Newgate Street
Road past the Goff's Oak PH. Turn right into Crouch Lane
and left into Rags Lane at the T junction. At the
roundabout take the second exit into Peakes Lane and
then right onto Hammond Street Road, left onto Holbeck
Lane and right into Appleby Street. A left turn **(25km)** into
Paradise Park Lane brings you - thankfully - onto the line
of Ermine Street. Over a couple of hills on tarmac then
straight on up a narrow unmade lane marked Ermine
Street and heavily cut with hoof prints. Soft going, hard
work especially after wet weather. Turn right on White

Stubbs Lane and left onto the now metalled Ermine Street. At the junction with Pembridge Lane this road swings left away from the Ermine Street line. Go right into the trees **(28km)** and descend the rough path to cross Cock Lane. Go on through the Martin's Green car park down into the woods and over the stream running east to feed the River Lee.

Important Roman roads like this one heading north from the Thames crossing to Lincoln, York and the Scotland were 24 feet wide often on a raised embankment called an agger. The surface was of fine stone chippings.

The broad green path known here as Red Hills continues on the Roman Line to cross Mangrove Lane. North of Mangrove Lane resist the temptation to use the drive to the farm, which runs parallel to the softer green gallop over a fence on the right. At the end of Box Wood this turns into a firm dirt road before reverting to a woodland path on the western edge of Elbow Lane Woods nature reserve.

Ermine Street emerges on to the B1197 at Hertford Heath **(32km)**. Turn left and then second right up into the village. Beyond the village green turn left to descend into the Lee Valley which has swung round and now runs east-west. Bend right at the bottom of the hill turning right onto the B502 then left to flyover the A414 and complete the descent into Ware. A left and (illegal to ride) right turn takes you into the High Street **(35 km)**. The station has trains for Liverpool Street (change at Broxbourne). The

Lee Navigation path will take you (left) to Hertford or
(right) back towards London.

*Ware was once prosperous brewing and malting centre. A mile
to the East is the village of Great Amwell where a glorious 18th
Century water garden stands on the New River complete with
a heroic monument to its creator . To the West between Ware
and Hertford are the open lands of King's Meads where the New
River takes water from the Lee. Its primary source, Chadwell
Springs, are seen best from the Ware/Hertford Road (A119)
opposite the entrance to Chadwell Springs Golf Club.*

18 KINGS CROSS TO WALTHAM CROSS

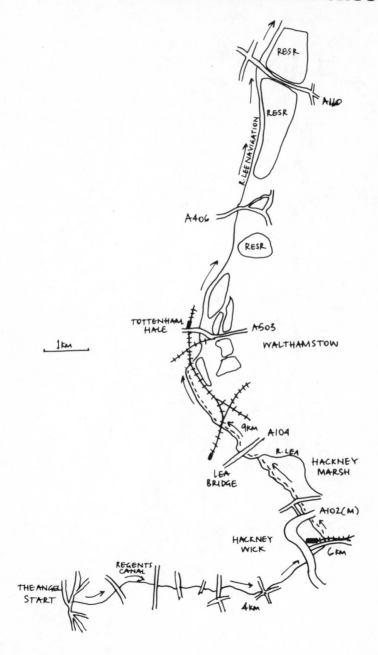

18 KINGS CROSS TO WALTHAM CROSS

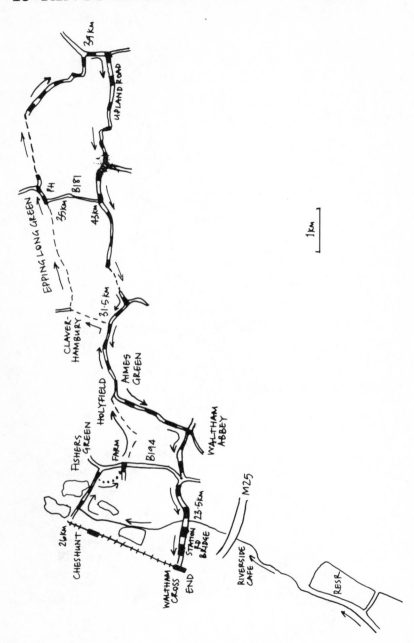

18 KINGS CROSS TO WALTHAM CROSS
The Lee Navigation and Epping Long Green

Maps   OS Landranger 177 East London, 166 Luton and Hertford, 167 Chelmsford.

From   The Angel Islington.

To   Waltham Abbey in Essex via Epping Long Green.

Distance 53km. Off-road 38km.

Route   From the foot of the Great North Road we follow waterways - excavated and improved - through inner London and out up the Hertfordshire/Essex border before turning east to make a loop on an old drovers track. The towing-path is almost all easy and well surfaced. The loop into Essex is dirty and arduous in places, particularly after wet weather.

Railway Access
    BR Stations Kings Cross (mainline or Thames Link) St. Pancras, Tottenham Hale and Waltham Cross. Information 071 928 5100.

Places of Interest
    Canal Museum - New Wharf Road N1.

    Walthamstow Marshes - in the Lea Valley.

150

Victoria Park - on the Hackney/Tower
Hamlets border.

Waltham Abbey.

Food and Drink
Many cafes in Upper Street.

Cafe - Springfield Park, Hackney.

Riverside Cafe, Ramney Marsh.

Cock and Magpie Pub, Epping Green.

Cross Keys Cafe, Thornwood Common.

The Angel Islington is an important historic route centre. Paths leading north from the City and West End - Goswell Road and St. John Street - meet here and were joined in the mid Eighteenth Century by the new City and Pentonville Roads. Just beyond at Islington Green, Islington Upper Street is the 'Great North Road' while the Essex Road diverges to the north east. In the pre-railway era this was where passengers caught coaches for the north and for those coming south (as Dickens observed in Oliver Twist) London began. Beneath the hill the Regents' Canal which links the Grand Union at Paddington to the Docks at Limehouse runs in tunnel. The small Canal Museum in Wharfedale Road (off New Wharf Road between York Way and Caledonian Road near the tunnel's Western portal) makes an excellent start (or finish) to the trip.

From the ridge-top boulevard of Upper Street descend eastwards on Charlton Place through the Camden Passage area, a busy antique market. Turn right into Colebrooke Row then left down Vincent Terrace to find the entry to the canal at the north end of the bridge on Danbury Street between Noel Road and Vincent Terrace. The water to the west is private mooring for house-boats. Continue east descending by City Road Lock to pass from Islington into Hackney.

The commercial traffic on the Regents Canal persisted longer than on rural waterways. After long distance freight transferred to the railways it was still busy with coal for the gas-works, timber for construction and beer for waterside pubs coming up from the Thames. Anyone who uses this towing path regularly will find the short 1920's silent film 'Barging through London' exhibited permanently at the London Canal Museum surprisingly familiar.

Beyond the Kingsland Basin and Broadway Market (interchange Route 1 Breathing Spaces) the Canal picks up and follows the perimeter of Victoria Park and bifurcates **(4km)** just beyond Old Ford Lock. The mainline continues south to the Docks. Turn left onto the Hertford Cut which continues along the edge of the Park to join the Lea Navigation at Hackney Wick. Just after the canal and river meet **(6km)** cross the road bridge to continue up the Lea valley on the Eastern side.

The River Lea has been channelled into a variety of streams over the years to power industry, drain its flat and marshy valley, and to form a corridor for water-traffic. As a barrier to land travel it has long been a significant political boundary first between Middlesex and Essex then London and Essex. This section is now Greater London on both banks. To your right is Hackney Marshes and the largest collection of football pitches in Europe.

Cross to the western bank beyond Hackney Marshes opposite the derelict power station. Having passed under the Lea Bridge Road cross to the east bank on the footbridge **(9km)** through the first of a succession of 'Stymie Gates' designed to contain motor-cycles.

On your right sports fields give way to Walthamstow Marsh which has never been drained, built on or cultivated - a rare site on the fringes of Inner London. There is a cafe here by the Rowing Club.

Cross to the western bank on the footbridge at Springfield Marina and continue north on the west bank.

The earthworks of Markfield Recreation Ground resemble iron-age fortifications but are in fact the remains of a disused Sewage Works.

Beyond the Ferry Lane bridge (where you can divert to Tottenham Hale BR Station) The path runs between a drainage channel and the Navigation before crossing to the east bank at Stonebridge Lock.

From here north the Valley is lined with reservoirs which

supply one sixth of London's fresh water. The grass on the banks is kept short by sheep, giving the area an incongruous upland flavour.

The Kingsway industrial estate precedes the North Circular road **(15km)**. Take care as heavy lorries use this access road. Go under the concrete bridge and press on past Picketts Lock and Ponders End to Enfield Lock. Cross to the west bank at the rifle factory entrance and continue onto Ramney Marsh.

The former weapons-factory is the home of the once ubiquitous Lee Enfield Rifle. The extensive site has been sold and is at present disused.

Pass the Riverside Cafe and go under the M25. The next bridge is Station Road **(23.5km)**. Turn right onto the road if you want to get straight to Waltham Abbey and cut out the Fisher's Green section. Find the B194 (signposted for Nazeing) Crooked Mile and follow it to rejoin the route at Monkham's Farm.

Having left Greater London the Lea is now the border between Herts and Essex represented here by Waltham Cross on the Hertford Road and Waltham Abbey in Essex. As late as the 1950's the bridge was the site of gang-fights between boys from the rival regions. Waltham Abbey has a compact centre about a kilometre from the Navigation. The Abbey is in ruins. Beyond Waltham abbey the neat reservoirs give way to wilder flooded gravel pits.

At the signpost **(26km)** for Cheshunt and Fisher's Green cross the navigation and keep right at the triangular green to cross the long bridge to reach a car-park. Exit onto Fishers Green Lane and just over the Cornmill Stream opposite the houses turn right onto the footpath that follows the field's edge. Continue round the high chain-link fence of the Government Research Station and pass through a gap in the hedge to emerge into Cornmill meadows. Turn left to come up to the Crooked Mile (B194) at Holyfield. Cross the road to **(28km)** take the bridleway (Clapgate Lane) signposted for Ames Green which begins at Monkham's Farm. Go straight on at the hilltop T junction to emerge at Ames Green **(30km)**.

Only one of the lanes through Ames Green has been improved for motors leaving the hamlet isolated at the foot of Galley Hill Wood, a northern out-post of Epping Forest.

Unless you want to explore Galley Hill keep to the right and on hitting tarmac turn left up the lane to Claverhambury. Pass Claverhambury Manor and opposite bungalows turn left **(31.5km)** onto the bridleway which runs along the edge of Deerpark Wood. This uphill field-edge gallop is difficult (for cyclists) in all conditions. The buildings on the skyline are Harold's Park Farm from where the going gets easier. On reaching the farm turn right to go round the big barn - actually an indoor menage (horse arena) - then right again to pick up the line of Epping Long Green.

Epping Long Green is a drovers track running in from Essex to the Lea Valley. It is administered by the Corporation of London who hold many of the ancient commons of London and environs in trust.

At the triangulation point (a little concrete bollard used in surveying) the old line of the path has been diverted. Turn left and right at the bottom of the field. At the corner of the field follow the track into the trees and then immediate right, through the hedge and straight on past Peacock's Farm to **(35km)** the junction of the Long Green and the Epping-Roydon Road (B 181).

Two big pubs serve food (Traveller's Friend specifies 'smart dress essential' which excludes anyone who came up Clapgate Lane - unless after a long drought). The Cock and Magpie dating from 1787 is friendlier. Two big pubs in the little village of Epping Green suggest that this was once an important crossroads.

The Long Green shares the line of the B181 for a few yards before continuing behind a pile of gravel. Despite its hilltop line this section is liable to deep flooding, after wet weather it does a passable impression of the Darien Gap. During the wet Winter of 1993/4 it held ponds four feet deep - take care. When the Long Green opens into a meadow keep to the left. Scorch marks from old fires and piles of builders waste tell you that you are nearing the motor-road. On reaching tarmac turn right. Follow this lane to join the old A11 (B1393) at Thornwood Common **(39km)**. Turn left to visit the Cross Keys Cafe (a notorious cyclists hangout - intersection Breathing Spaces The

Roding & The Cam Ride) otherwise turn right then right again into Upland Road.

The broad skies wooden barns and duck ponds of this section gives a taste of the scenery of the Essex Lanes. The rare breed centre at Essingbury Farm has a cafe open-all year round.

The B181 merges up from the left. When the road turns right **(43km)** carry straight on past the No-Through-Road Sign. Tarmac finishes after 1km, continue on a green road. Beyond the horse-stile reach a T junction turn right (a left turn here leads to Upshire on the fringe of Epping Forest) to return through Claverhambury. At the turn for Ames Green **(48km)** (turn right if you want to retrace Clapgate Lane) keep straight on down Galley Hill Road. At the bottom by the Cobbins Brook Bridge turn right onto Parklands which brings you back to the big roundabout at Waltham Abbey. Left and right to explore the town, straight on to get to the Lea Navigation or Waltham Cross BR **(53km)**.

19 HERTS 'N' ESSEX

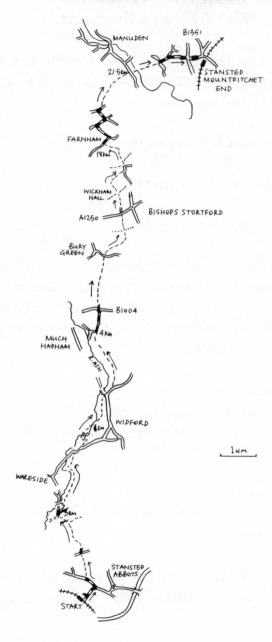

19 HERTS 'N' ESSEX
The Ash and the Stort

Maps   OS Landranger 166 Luton and Hertford (first 4kms only), 167 Chelmsford, Harlow and surrounding area.

From   Stansted St Margarets.

To   Stansted Mountfitchet.

Distance 24km. Off-road 18km.

Route   Up the meandering banks of the Ash on long neglected green roads through pasture and woods to Much Hadham. Then climbing on rougher tracks over the cornfields of Essex before reaching the busy hilltop town of Stansted Mountfitchet.

Railway Access
> BR Stations St. Margarets, Stansted Mountfitchet trains from Liverpool Street. Information 071 928 5100.

Places of Interest
> Widford Church - ancient church with wall paintings.
>
> Hadham Forge - Much Hadham cottage museum of rural life and working forge.

Stanstead Mountfitchet - hilltop town with a
replica Motte and Bailey castle on the site of a
real one.

Food and Drink
The Bull PH, Much Hadham.

The Mill Tea-rooms, Chip Shop, among others
at Stanstead Mountfitchet.

From St. Margarets Station turn left and cross the Lee
Navigation. (You can also reach this point by coming
north on the tow path from Broxbourne or east from Ware
or Hertford.) Continue into the brick-paved High Street
of Stanstead Abbots. Pass Cheers Bar and a Bakers Shop
with a cafe in the rear. When the High Street bends right
turn left onto Cappell Lane. Pass St Andrews Church as
the Lee valley opens to the left. Dead opposite the 1906
semis of Amherst Villas turn right into the unpromising
garage forecourt that becomes a rising bridleway - signposted Wareside - across meadows. Go straight on at the
bridleway crossroads. The path passes woods on the right.
As it sweeps to the left and the land ahead falls away to
the river, fork to the right along the edge of the wood.

*The brick clock tower on the corner of Cappell Lane is the Old
Clock School built in 1636 and designed by Sir Edward Baeshe.
The lonely crossroads of unmade roads between Stansted Abbots
and Wareside is a reminder of the days when agriculture
demanded much more labour and most travel was local and on
foot. The dense network of paths and tracks were all in daily*

use as cottagers, labourers and farmers moved between home and the fields, church and market.

At the pink, tile-roofed cottage go straight ahead on a single track - following the line of the telephone cables - make the first (of many) crossing of the Ash on the little wooden bridge **(3km)**. Hard cases can use the horse path down to ford the river. Climb to the brick bridge then turn right down to cross the river again and make an immediate left through a rusty gate.

As the Ash meanders through the meadows the old line of the road can just be discerned as a shallow eroded gully. The dense network of paths used by the much larger rural population who needed to walk a direct line meant that long distance traffic - this was once a main route to Cambridge - could choose their route depending on the state of a range of parallel routes. Often a single route only emerge when all weather surfaces became widespread.

Two gates further on cross the river on a concrete bridge. Go through the metal gate onto the disused railway track-bed and turn right. Follow this until it is blocked. Fork right to follow the fields edge uphill. Turn left into the woods on a single track (easy to miss) which brings you out on the B1004 opposite the gate of Blakesware Manor. Turn right on the road. Turn left into the entrance of the coke depot and right onto the chestnut avenue beyond the gate. Cross the river on the dilapidated brick and iron bridge.

The Church Spire on the low hill to the right is St. John the Baptist Widford. Parts of it have stood above the Ash since at least the 13th Century. It contains 14th Century wall paintings.

A fence with a stile announces a short footpath section. Cross to the path and walk right along the fields edge. Cross the river on the stiled footbridge **(6.5km)**. Turn left, cross another style and turn left on a fenced bridle path (turn right here if you want to visit Widford Church). Reach the road and cross over to go up the concrete drive of the pumping station. Just before you reach it turn left onto a bridleway.

Don't miss the metal plaque in the hedge on the left explaining how the path was widened.

On reaching the main road (B180) up the Ash valley cross it and then turn left into the Hadham Towers gravel depot. Beyond the weighbridge and huge gravel bins go on into the woods along the valley. Sometimes the path gets very boggy and there are diversions up into the woods. The last section is cruelly cramped between barbed wire and brambles which in August and September are loaded with blackberries. On reaching the road **(9km)** turn left. If you are going on turn right when the road bears left. If you wish to visit Much Hadham keep left. At the ford cross the river (There is a footbridge for the faint hearted) and turn right. This is the back lane of Much Hadham and emerges into the High Street opposite the Bull PH and the Forge.

Much Hadham is one of those places (like Castle Acre or Godstone) which was once more important than it is now. Its ribbon development contains many grand 18th Century houses and a palace - this was a residence of the Bishop of London from the 10th Century. There are also humble old buildings, houses, cottages, shops and pubs. The Forge is still working and houses a museum of country life which is open on Saturdays and Sundays. A nineteenth country cottage garden is replicated at the back. Henry Moore who lived in the area until his death in 1986 donated to sculptures which stand in the churchyard.

If you have been into the village retrace to rejoin the route and continue to Dane Bridge. Turn right over the bridge and then left on to the bridle path. When a path joins from the right turn left then right and carry on along the line of the telephone wires. Cross a farm road and carry on along the line of the brook. Pass the woods and follow the line of the big power pylons. Pass under the A120 **(14.5km)**.

There is a short section of unimproved 'A' road preserved beyond the new flyover for the A120.

Go on up the drive ahead and just before the house turn right and follow the timber fence round to the woods. Keep left then right and go on with a large area of woodland on your left and a smaller one on the right. On meeting a gravel farm road turn right. At the farmyard turn left on the concrete road. Pass the communication mast. Turn left then follow the edge of the woods heading towards Farnham Church which can be seen ahead.

As the route crosses the county boundary the metal finger Bridle Way posts of Herts are replaced by the concrete ones of Essex.

At the bottom of the hill turn left at the T junction of paths and climb to the road. Turn right then left at the triangular green **(17.5km)**. Turn right by the village hall, then left at the next T junction. Turn right at the next T junction and then fork left past the concrete bridleway post. Take the gate to the right marked 'bridleway' to take a line past the stag head oak to find a gate at the bottom corner of the field. Go through it and turn left on an overgrown path through a strip of tall beechwoods.

The path switches to the edge of the field on the left by a lone gate post. Carry on with the woods on your left and the field on your right. Sometimes the field is ploughed right up to the overgrown strip at the edge making the going difficult. When the line of the woodland edge swings left across your path rurn right onto the green track through the trees. Emerge form the woods and descend to a lane make a right left dog leg **(21km)** and continue on the bridle way. On meeting a track turn left and then right towards the finger post you can see across the meadow. Turn left on the road then right. Keep right at Bentfield Green onto Bentfield Causeway then turn right into Bentfield Road. Cross the old A11 and descend to find the Norman Castle, Toy Museum and station **(23km)** at the bottom of town. The Mill House Tea Room is to the left in Lower Road.

The Motte and Bailey Castle is given a slightly comic aspect by the colourful signs to entice visitors. This is a refreshing contrast to the usual rather dry and respectful treatment and packaging of ancient monuments. The Animated Toy Museum next door claims to be one of the largest and most comprehensive toy collections in the country.

If you have the pluck and daylight, or just a lot of pluck you can take the old A11 down to Stortford and pick up the footpath beside the Stort Navigation which will take you back to the river Lee via Sawbridgeworth and Harlow converting this into a circular ride of three rivers.

20 THE PEDDARS WAY

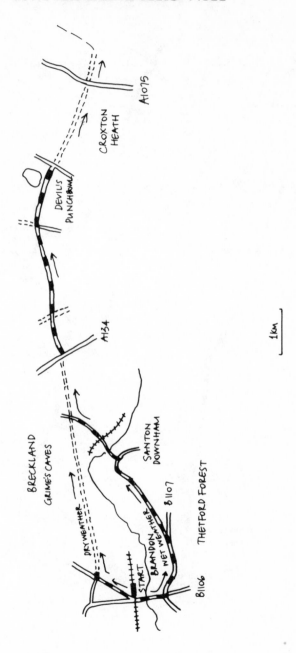

20 THE PEDDARS WAY

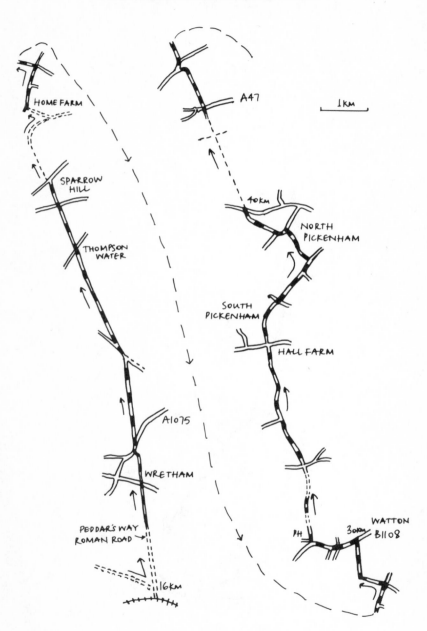

HOME FARM

A47

1 KM

SPARROW HILL

THOMPSON WATER

40 KM

NORTH PICKENHAM

SOUTH PICKENHAM

HALL FARM

A1075

WRETHAM

PEDDAR'S WAY ROMAN ROAD

16 KM

PH

WATTON B1108

30 KM

20 THE PEDDARS WAY

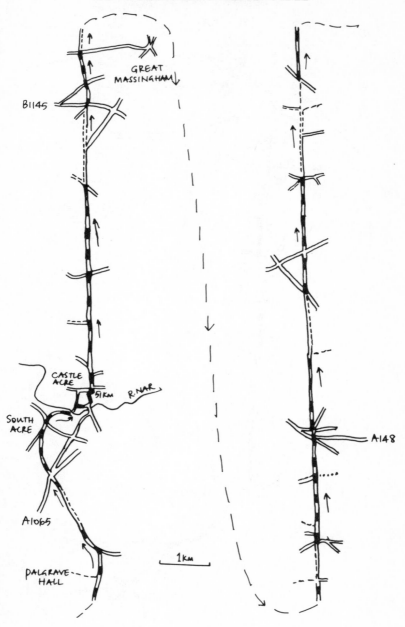

GREAT MASSINGHAM

B1145

CASTLE ACRE

51 KM

R. NAR

SOUTH ACRE

A1065

PALGRAVE HALL

A148

1 KM

20 THE PEDDARS WAY

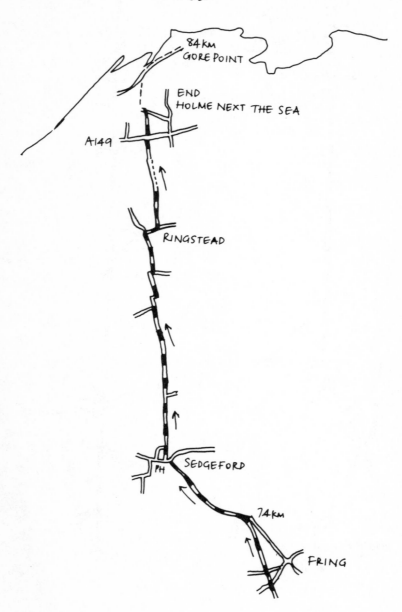

THE SEA

84 KM
GORE POINT

END
HOLME NEXT THE SEA

A149

RINGSTEAD

PH   SEDGEFORD

74 KM

FRING

20 THE PEDDARS WAY
Across West Norfolk

Maps   OS Landranger 144 Thetford and Breckland, 132 North West Norfolk.

From   Brandon on the Suffolk Border.

To   Holme next the Sea on the Norfolk Coast.

Distance 84km. Off-road 43km.

Route   This ancient trackway offers an extended and remote itinerary. As a two day trip it is suitable for mixed ability groups, taken in a single stage it will challenge fit and experienced riders. The surface is firm and well drained, passable even in the wettest weather although some sections may hold large puddles. The ride is not flat but since it hardly rises above 300m hills are either steep or long but never both. The section north of Castle Acre is exposed and head-winds can make the going very difficult.

Railway Access
Brandon Station with trains from London Liverpool Street. Kings Lynn is the nearest station to Holme next the Sea.

Places of Interest
Grimes Graves - prehistoric flint mines near Brandon.

Thetford Forest - a mountain bike playground near Brandon.

Castle Acre - historic Norfolk village with spectacular medieval ruins.

The seaside.

Accommodation
YHA Brandon 0842 812075.

The Old Red Lion Staging House, Castle Acre 0760 755557 (obvious half way stop).

Food and Drink
Pubs and Cafes - Brandon, Swaffham and Castle Acre.

Pubs, Wretham, Little Cressingham, Sedgeford and Ringstead.

Shops in Wretham, North Pickenham, Castle Acre, Ringstead and Holme next the Sea.

Brandon stands on the Little Ouse river, where it forms the Norfolk/Suffolk border. It is the centre of Breckland an area of sandy heath deforested in the New Stone Age when the flint industry boomed. In modern times conifer trees have been planted, initially to stabilise the light soil and later for commercial forestry. Thetford Forest, which extends south and east of Brandon, contains miles of tracks open to bikes (info.

0842 810271). Mtbs can be hired from Brandon Youth Hostel.

Leave Brandon heading north (up the High Street away from the river) and fork right onto the A1065 signed for Swaffham. After about **1km** a metalled lane emerges from the left and continues to the right as a sandy forest track. This is Harling Drove, turn right and follow it.

You can visit the ancient flint mines at Grimes Graves by continuing 2kms north on the A1065 and turning right. The Drove is a very old highway, certainly pre-Roman. It probably started in the fens and ran out to the North Sea coast.

The first section of Harling Drove undulates and can be hard going after wet weather if heavy Forestry Commission plant has been operating in the area. For an easier start take the B1107 east out of Brandon, fork left to cross the Little Ouse at Santon Downham and 1km beyond the river turn right onto the sandy forest track as it crosses the lane.

After crossing a metalled lane (where the short cut rejoins), Harling Drove crosses the A134 and continues as a quiet road, before returning to trackway and going on to cross the A1075 on Wretham Heath.

Harling Drove passes a succession of Breckland meres; the Devils Punchbowl, Fowl Mere, Ringmere and Langmere. Watering places are rare on the fast draining sand and these may account for the line of this drovers path.

After a brief interlude in open country the path returns to forest. It meets the Peddars Way by a level-crossing on the Norwich/Ely Railway **(16km)**. Turn sharp left to begin the long trek north. The track crosses a lane then makes a sharp left under the disused Thetford-Swaffham railway and right on the A1075 to pass through Wretham where there is a Post Office-shop and a pub. Beyond the village fork left onto a minor road. The path now passes through a military training area with Danger signs on both sides.

The Peddars Way may have been in use before the Romans straightened and unified it. Ancient British tracks tended to have several alternate lines.

Follow the Peddars Way signs as the lane becomes a track running close by the artificial lake and nature reserve of Thompson Water. The rubble track becomes grassy single-track as it skirts the Merton Park Estate. This section needs careful navigation as the Roman line is lost. Over a wooden step-stile for horses the path runs onto farm roads. Pass Home Farm then turn left onto a green lane which emerges into the busy B1108 **(30km)**. Turn left for Little Cressingham. Fork right into the village then turn right onto the lane called Peddars Way. The White Horse PH serves food and has warming fires in Winter.

Follow this lane over two crossroads leaving the official line of the path (unsuitable for bikes as it zig-zags on footpaths across the valley of the river Wissey) before turning left into North Pickenham. In North Pickenham turn left and follow the road as it sweeps to the right. At the T junction go straight ahead through the disused railway bridge on green Procession Lane **(40km)**.

A left turn at the crossing of tracks beyond North Pickenham will take you into Swaffham, a lively and well preserved market-town with pubs, cafes and a chip-shop. The Saturday auctions of animals, furniture and old bikes are a highlight.

Cross the fast and busy A47 and continue on a lane to make a third abandoned railway crossing. Turn right, then left onto the farm road which continues to Great Palgrave where a left turn takes the road down to cross the A1065 at a staggered junction. This lane climbs to South Acre where the right fork marked FORD UNSUITABLE FOR MOTORS leads down to the river Nar. The ford has a footbridge but can be ridden depending on the courage of the rider and height of the water. Turn right then follow the road up to the left as it climbs the narrow village street to the castle gate **(51km)**.

Castle Acre is a curiosity. A small village off the current main road system. It is surrounded by a huge complex of ruins. The Monastery by the river is imposing even in its roofless state and the Norman castle whose walls enclosed much of the present day village has left fragmentary ruins and grand earth-works. Castle Acre was a last stop on the pilgrim road to Walsingham and the largest of a complex of monasteries in the Nar valley, the 'Norfolk Holly Land'.

Turn right on the High Street then left to leave the village on the Great Massingham road. North of Castle Acre navigation is very easy as the Way follows a dead straight line the first 4.5kms on road then onto tracks of varying quality. Close to the village of Fring the path passes an isolated house surrounded by trees at the next road **(74km)** the path continues up a footpath so cyclists need to detour left into Sedgeford. Turn second right in the village (go a little further ahead if you want to visit the William IVth which serves food) to continue North to Ringstead. Pass through Ringstead and a right and left turn brings you back onto the line of the Peddars Way. After two more kilometres go straight across the A149 and into Holme Next the Sea whose main street runs parallel to the coast. Go through a gate and cross a meadow to reach the coast road and the dunes and flats of Gore Point **(84km)**.

The ride finishes on a sweep of coast where the Wash and North Sea meet. Big sky and water on three sides the end of the Earth. Roman travellers would embark here to cross into Lincolnshire and continue up the country.

The railway to Hunstanton, (4kms west of the finish and locally pronounced 'Hunston' - a rather dismal 19th Century resort) was dismantled long ago. To reach the rail-head you must ride back to Kings Lynn. The best route is to retrace to Sedgeford then via Ingoldisthorpe, Sandringham and Castle Rising. Trains: Brandon Station is served by trains running between Ely and Norwich. Kings Lynn has good connections to London and the East Coast Main Line.